Powered From Within:

Stories About Running & Triathlon

Margreet Dietz

www.margreetdietz.com

Cover image: © Margreet Dietz

Author image: © Timothy Moore

ISBN 978 1 4499906 0 2

Also by Margreet Dietz

Running Shoes Are a Girl's Best Friend

ACKNOWLEDGEMENTS

This book is a collection of articles I wrote for magazines in Australia and Canada. I thank the editors and publishers for the opportunity to write about the power running and triathlon have brought to the people who have the courage to try these sports.

At Run For Your Life I thank publisher Daniel Green and editorial content manager Lennon Wicks. At Australian Triathlete I thank Amy White who was then its editor. At Canadian Running I thank editor-in-chief Michal Kapral. At Canada's IMPACT Magazine I thank editor Jay Winans and publisher Elaine Kupser.

The runners and triathletes I interviewed for these stories left me with a better understanding of what it means to be an endurance athlete, professional or amateur. They inspired me - as I hope they will you. I thank Craig Alexander and his wife Nerida, Gerrard Gosens and his wife Heather, Alan Farrell and his wife Carole, Bernie Millett, Ron Stuart, Stephen Callahan, Brian McCarthy, Tony McClement, Joe Esposito and his partner Mia Ursini, Kenneth Lewis, Tim A'hern, Shelley Maxwell-Smith, Karen Scott, Zoe King, Kate Rowe, Kristian Manietta, Charlotte Paul, Tess Waterhouse, Liz Swinton, Sam Bellgardt, Nick Munting, Stephen Bourdeau, Kevin Smith and Dave Scott-Thomas.

Last but not least, I thank my partner Tim Moore for his support in shaping most of these stories.

CONTENTS

CHAPTER 1

Australian Lucy Alexander, who turned four in May, is spending her fifth summer in Boulder, Colorado, which is home to many triathletes including six-time Ironman World Champion Dave Scott. She is already a frequent long-haul flyer who knows to ask flight attendants for extra pillows and blankets, and understands exactly how to operate her personal TV screen. "She thinks everyone goes to the airport and goes for long trips on a plane. She thinks that's normal," says her dad, Craig Alexander, in a telephone interview from Boulder, where the family is based for about four months of the year.

What also seems normal to Lucy is that Dad wins almost every triathlon he enters. She was born in 2005, a couple of months before Craig won the Life Time Fitness Triathlon, one of the richest triathlons in the world consisting of a 1.5-kilometre swim, a 40- kilometre bike, and a 10-kilometre run. He's been on a tear ever since.

In 2006 Craig became the inaugural Ford Ironman 70.3 World Champion (1.9-kilometre swim, ninety-kilometre bike, 21.1-kilometre run) and posted a slew of other impressive results that saw him chosen as *Triathlete Magazine*'s Triathlete of the Year. In 2007 he started his first Ford Ironman World Championship (3.8-kilometre swim, 180.1-kilometre bike, 42.195-kilometre run) in Kona, Hawaii, to finish an incredible second. There was only one place to go in 2008, and Lucy was the first to hug her dad at the finish line after he became the Ironman World Champion. "My daughter will tell everyone who will listen that her dad is an Ironman Champion. She knows what it is all about as she's grown up with it," Craig says.

Dad sometimes worries he has set the bar a bit too high for his little girl. "In some ways I feel bad because so many races since she has been alive I have won; I think she just expects that is what happens. Hopefully she will remember that Dad was someone who worked hard and tried hard because that is what I would like her to remember."

Hard work and the unwavering support of his wife Nerida are exactly how this 36-year-old Australian has managed to become one of the most successful and versatile triathletes in a now ten-year professional career, which started relatively late. Initially a short-course triathlete, he only tried his hand at the Ironman distance in 2007. People had high expectations for him and Alexander didn't disappoint. His main objective this year is to defend his Ironman World Champion title—a challenging goal. In the Hawaii Ironman's thirty-year history only three men have been able to win in consecutive years: Dave Scott, Mark Allen, and Tim DeBoom. "Once you've won a race, unless you're going to do that again, it's not the same," Craig says.

If his early results this season are any indication, he's on track for another stellar performance in Kona. Craig has won three

Ironman 70.3 races in 2009: Geelong, Australia; Singapore; and Hawaii. "So far it has been a great year. I see no reason why that is not going to continue. I've been training hard and I am in good shape," says Craig, who loves racing the half-Ironman distance.

The win at the Hawaii 70.3 came just five weeks after son Austin was born—it's not just Lucy who will equate Dad with crossing the line first. In the eight weeks leading up to Austin's birth, Craig took a break from racing and used the time to work hard on his perceived weakness, cycling. With a minimum of 450 kilometres of cycling a week, Craig has pushed towards the 700-kilometre mark for several weeks in the last few months.

"I felt I was already at a high level on the bike. Obviously in the Ironman you ride 180 kilometres, so coming from a short-course background I felt that is the area where I most needed to improve. Time-wise it is the largest part of the race, so it's a place where you can make up the most time but also lose the most time," he says.

Part of the motivation to focus on his cycling endurance and strength is the fact that he has posted some of the fastest run splits in Kona and the sport. He ran a 2:45 marathon in his first and second appearances in Hawaii. "If you're perceived as one of the best runners in the race, then people think you are not strong at anything else. That is a fallacy—you need to be strong in all three (disciplines) to win. I perceive that my competition feel that there is a weakness on the bike, and I feel that is where I am going to be attacked this year. So I am just shoring up that aspect of my race," Craig says.

Don't for a moment think he's neglecting his run. Craig says he believes he can improve his running too. "It all works hand in hand because I think the stronger you are on the bike and the more efficient you are on the bike, the more energy you have for the run anyway. So not only do you ride quicker but you also ride more efficiently."

Craig, who has a bachelor of applied science in physiotherapy but laughs when asked about his stretching routine, writes his own training programs. However, he has always sought the help of others including Ironman legend Dave Scott and Victoria's LifeSport master coach Lance Watson, who has guided the likes of Simon Whitfield. Scott has provided a wealth of information and advice to Craig, who's not the least bit shy about asking for it.

"If I am sitting next to someone like Dave Scott on the pool deck and I've got a question to ask, well, I am going to ask someone I think knows the answer. It all comes back to being a professional and doing everything you can to get the outcome that you want. Dave has been really generous with me and always been more than willing to help me. Some days I just hit him with question after question and he answers them all. He has been a massive, massive benefit to me," Craig says.

As he made the move to Iron-distance races, Craig sought more structured advice. In 2007 he was introduced to Chris Carmichael, Lance Armstrong's coach, and now works closely with Nick White, a coach at Carmichael Training Systems. "Nick is a very knowledgeable guy. He knows he doesn't need to look over my shoulder every day, and we certainly don't speak every day—not even close. But I know that any time I need a question answered, I can ring Nick and get great advice. I have a power metre on my bike, and most of the rides I download the data for Nick, so Nick certainly oversees pretty much every bike session."

Craig is a professional in every sense. "If you're going to make the commitment to do all this training and spend all this money to do all these races, and live overseas for six months, it's your duty to do everything you can to make it a successful campaign. That doesn't mean you have to win."

Contrary to popular belief, he doesn't assess his season based on Kona, and he doesn't consider having won in Kona last year as a reason in itself to celebrate. "In my mind, the performance was far from perfect. I can improve a lot on it."

Craig says his Hawaiian victory represents "a successful campaign because I trained hard physically, I mentally prepared well, and I did my homework. My preparation was very good—

that's why, in my mind, that whole campaign and that race was a success. As long as I can say I did everything I could, that's important. It's not the winning or losing that keeps you awake; it's maximizing your potential and executing a great performance that you know you're capable of. The fact that I won it is a massive bonus, obviously. For me, a great season is not just one race.

"If you look over the history of our sport, the best athletes over any distance have been consistent over a whole season. Even now, you look at ITU racing, guys like [Simon] Whitfield and [Bevan] Docherty just keep it going year after year for the whole season. It's the same in Olympic distance non-drafting, Craig Walton was the same, and also when you step up to Ironman: guys like Normann [Stadler] - he is rarely out of the top five when he is not sick or injured. When I came into the sport I modelled myself on the top guys at the time. You look at who's the best and why they are the best. I used to like the guys who would win, obviously, and I liked the guys who could win in different conditions: non-drafting or drafting, hilly bike ride or flat bike.

"And I used to like the guys who were consistent. That's what you model yourself on, and I guess you aspire to that sort of level yourself. It's funny, getting back to the goal for this year, it has to be Kona, as that's what everyone is going to judge it on. But for me, I always judge a year on its entirety, not on just one race. That being said, Kona is the jewel in the crown, for sure."

Craig says he doesn't over-analyse his rivals. "I do think about them a little bit in training. I like to think about myself and what I need to do. We've all raced each other enough times over different distances - everyone knows everyone's strengths and weaknesses and the way people tend to race."

While the pressure is sure to be high on him in Kona on October 10th, 2009, Craig says he isn't fazed by it. "There's always pressure. When you train hard and you expect big things of yourself - I mean I put a lot of pressure on myself. I know what I expect and it will be the same. There will be pressure this year."

Craig says his focus is on his preparation: "You're nervous before every big race, but I think I try to take that out of the game as much as possible by just preparing as best as I can in the months leading up. "If you're sitting there on race week thinking: physically I have done everything on my program that I had to do; mentally I am up for it—I am ready, I am motivated to go. You feel like you have done your homework. I think that alleviates a little bit of the pressure because it's not like you're walking into an exam thinking, I haven't studied."

He also credits his wife with reminding him of his love for the sport at times when pre-race anxiety builds. "A lot of the pressure comes with the fact that it is your job, but the reason you started in the sport is that you had a passion for it and you loved it. My wife is very good at helping me remember that and she is probably the greatest asset I've got because she takes a lot of the stress out of it for me. She deals with the sponsors, the media, and all I have to deal with is the race - that's it."

Craig also often thinks of his family during races, as he wants to make the sacrifices they make to support his career worthwhile. It helps him focus on the goal - getting to the finish line first. Knowing what it took to get there is what makes winning so sweet each time he does. "Every single race I win I get an immense joy out of because that is why you do it."

Craig stresses the importance of keeping a perspective in the week leading up to Kona and any other key goal race for professional and amateur athletes alike. "The main thing is just don't lose your head. People tend to lose their head in that last week and overtrain or get nervous. Have faith in your level of ability, firstly, and have faith in your build-up, in what you've done, and then just go out and express your fitness on race day. Once you get into race week, it's too late to start worrying about a lack of fitness. That had to be worried about a few months ago. That's my mantra: worry about it when it needs to be worried about. I try to turn it around a bit and think, Hawaii is a great race. It is a great day. It is one of the pinnacle races of our sport and this is where I want to be. You've put yourself in this situation so there is no point worrying about it and being nervous about it. This is excitement. This is what it is all about."

Craig says he takes nothing for granted. "There are no guarantees in sport—you can't go there expecting to win. You can go there thinking 'I am in great shape and I am going to be competitive.' Twenty years from now I am the only one who is going to remember my races there, so it is important for me to do it the right way and to be happy with what I've done."

(First published in IMPACT Magazine in 2009)

CHAPTER 2

If you're not living on the edge, you are taking up too much space is one of the favourite quotes of Gerrard Gosens, who completed his first marathon at the age of 17 and ran a 120-kilometre ultra from Rockhampton to Gladstone a few months later.

Now 38, he has just returned from competing in his third Paralympic Games and plans to be part of the London 2012 team. After that he'll resume his quest to climb Mt Everest. Not only does he train daily at an elite level, he also holds down a fulltime and high-profile job at Vision Australia and is married with two children. Gerrard, who was born blind, says he's never been the type to test the water first. "I suppose when I jump into something, I jump in with both feet," he says.

From a young age Gerrard's parents encouraged him to do the things other kids did, instead of deciding beforehand they'd be impossible because of his lack of sight. Gerrard rode his bicycle to school and was a tagger in an under-13 AFL team – which was also when he started running to achieve and maintain the fitness required for that role. (A tagger's job is to run around with the best player(s) of the other team and stifle their ability to win possession.) "Even though I couldn't see the ball, I could always hear it coming or hear a group of players. I rode my bike to school by following the sound of my brother's bike in front of me. And that was because my parents didn't put me in cotton wool and said, 'He's totally blind - don't ride a push bike, don't go ride a motorbike'. I did all those things. And they said, `It's better to have a go and see what happens'. That's where that thirst for life comes from. It's been about realising we have a very short time of life on earth and for me it is about making the most of the opportunities."

As Gerrard, an outstanding student, went to university he upped his run training. "It was an opportunity because there were a number of other people who were running so I could sort of come alongside them." Back then many people were not sure how to approach him, Gerrard says. "You'll find in my youth and back in the early 80s, it was probably the people in their late 30s or their 40s that were more relaxed with a person who had a physical disability. The younger generation would be, `Oh my god what do I do – that person's blind'."

Gerrard has always focused on finding ways to make things happen. "Many people will look at the obstacles, not the opportunities," he says. He decided that his marathon-running training partners provided him with an opportunity. "I thought, 'I am surrounded by people who run distances: where's the opportunity I can derive from this?' And that's what led to the marathon."

He devised his own programs by learning from his training partners as well as by reading about run training. "It was a matter of absorbing the information that surrounded me."

With Gerrard depending on having another person guide him on every run, he had to be flexible at times. "It was about what guide runners were around. You had to match up your guide runners to what their abilities were as well. You have to work with the resources that are there," Gerrard says.

And that is still what he does today. Robbie Bolton, national distance coach for Australia's Paralympic Committee, says, "It's a team approach with all athletes in my squad but particularly with Gerrard."

Gerrard's personal best (PB) times range from 4:21 for 1500m, 16:33 for 5000m, 74:55 for the half marathon and 2:52 for the marathon - that means his team of 12 guide runners must include elite athletes too. They have to be able to keep up, as well as be alert enough during an entire training session or race to point out any obstacles and potential dangers along the way.

Bruce Jones, who has coached Gerrard for the past four years and is one of his guide runners, says a guide runner must be able to run at least 10 seconds a kilometre faster than the person they're guiding. Gerrard says, "There are many guide runners that would struggle to keep up on the track with me. If they go within themselves to try to keep up or to try and keep their speed up, then obviously that is pretty dangerous because they have to be able to focus on two things simultaneously.

"So you know your range of guide runners obviously is a very narrow field of elite runners."

As Gerrard's profile has grown with his list of achievements and the profile of Paralympic athletes in general, it has allowed him to access more and better resources. Yet managing his team is an ongoing effort. "It always is a hard issue to find people to run with and he's still looking for another option as a top guide runner. He relies on his No. 1 guide runner [Dennis Fitzgerald] and if that person gets injured he's got to have reserves," Bruce says.

Ironically, Gerrard's first Paralympic Games in Atlanta in 1996 where he was part of the Australian goalball team left him deflated about team sport and prompted his return to athletics, Gerrard says. "We worked really hard and we got into the medal playoffs. We actually lost the playoff for the bronze medal and we came fourth in the world. One of my team members made a few errors in the early part of the game and for me personally that was very frustrating because they were simple mistakes that could have been prevented. After putting many, many years and obviously a lot of blood, sweat and tears into the sport, I came away thinking I had to be in charge of my own destiny."

When Gerrard returned from Atlanta, he hooked up with coach Ed Salmon and began training for the 5000m, 10,000m and the marathon for the 2000 Paralympic Games in Sydney.

"The funny thing about my life is that even though I left the team sport of goalball, I actually am always in a team. Every part of my life is team work, for example working with my guide dog is team work, going to the movies with my wife Heather is about team work."

Gerrard particularly credits Heather as one of the driving forces behind his accomplishments. "We have a perfect balance. You can do the article on Gerrard Gosens but behind Gerrard Gosens there is a very large team. There's a team called my wife and the balance is there to make that success happen," he says.

Gerrard's accomplishments so far will impress any runner, even more so when considering his complete lack of sight. Gerrard says he'd like others to appreciate the additional challenges he faces to achieve those results. "For example I absolutely envy any person who can wake up early in the morning, pull their shoes and their shorts on, and go for a run.

"That must be such an absolutely awesome feeling. Whereas I have to make sure that my guide runner is fit and turns up and that they're capable of running that distance and that their body's in shape for a hard workout or a recovery run. So there are a lot more fundamental pressures on training every single day of my life than there are for a person who is fully sighted. And then there is obviously the aspect of – and this is a subconscious thing – you as a runner can see how other people run. I actually can't do that. I actually have no physical conception of how they run as elite athletes," Gerrard says.

Gerrard competed in the 5000m, 10,000m and the marathon in the Sydney Paralympic Games in 2000. He learnt an important lesson there, which was that being rested both mentally and physically is crucial for elite athletes to perform their best.

While preparing for three events as an athlete, he was also working overtime in his job with the Australian Paralympic Committee.

"The Sydney 2000 Games for me were a challenge. I was probably my own worst enemy because I worked so hard to make sure the Games were successful yet sacrificed my own efforts as an athlete at the Games. By the time I got to the Village I was probably exhausted – I probably hadn't rested myself enough. I went into the 5000m - I was ranked No. 2 in the world - and the gun went and there was just nothing. I felt fit, but I was just mentally fatigued and that's where from a distance athlete's perspective you just have to have that mental freshness about you, not just that physical freshness."

Still, Gerrard finished sixth in the 5000m in a time of 17:27.01 and sixth in the 10,000m in 37:05.64. He ran the marathon in 3:03.18. "My performance at the Games was, I think, very good considering where I was at because back then I was always very conscious of making sure the Sydney Paralympic games were a success," he says.

The success of the Sydney Paralympic Games, as well as of those in Athens and Beijing, has changed a lot for athletes with a disability, Gerrard says. "This year [2008] has been probably the best-ever coverage of the Paralympic Games. I know people in Australia now who watched more Paralympic Games than they did the Olympics. Five to 10 years ago, it was unheard of – people actually sitting down and watching wheelchair basketball or athletics and certainly that level of understanding has reached a new level."

People have become more comfortable around people with a disability because of the Paralympic Games. "There isn't that much fear, that unknown of 'Oh my god do I say to Gerrard did you see that movie last week', or 'Gee doesn't that house look nice'. Ten years ago people would have thought 'Do I say the words *see* or *look*?' Whereas now, it is all very comfortable. That awareness, that understanding - not just about blindness but about paraplegy or cerebral palsy - has taken a new level," Gerrard says.

It has also boosted funding for the Paralympic athletes in general and for distance runners in particular, says Robbie. That, for example, allowed the Paralympic distance team to attend several altitude camps in Australia, a three-week altitude training in the south of France in preparation for Beijing and access to nutritionists, physiotherapists and sports psychologists.

There's more to be done. "We have had access to far more funds than we have had in the past. And that momentum needs to continue because we have got two 20-year-olds in the distance running squad. The other three are 35 and above. So we need to put some more money into the talent identification at the moment in those first few years leading up to London. There are other talented athletes out there but I guess aren't aware of the opportunities that are around in Paralympic sport and in Paralympic distance running at the moment. We really need to focus, particularly in the next one to two years, on finding those athletes so that we can prepare them for London. After that, in that two- to four-year intervening period, we need to get more professional and need to provide more opportunities so that the athletes maybe only need to work part-time, instead of fulltime, like some of their able-bodied counterparts do," Robbie says.

When Bruce became Gerrard's coach four years ago, he added speed sessions to his program, worked on improving his running style and took him to a sports psychologist to help his mental preparation. "He never really did speed work. He was basically just doing longer stuff. We started pretty much straightaway doing a lot more sprint work and a lot more track work," Bruce says.

Bruce and Gerrard also worked hard on improving his technique. "Gerrard seemed to run very heavy. I basically told him to stride out more. We did a lot of drills where we would do hill reps and then we'd also do drills while we were actually sprinting and I'd tell him to drive his arms higher and to drive his knees higher because he was running very low and he had to be on his toes more," Bruce says. They focused on his arm movements too. "When you run you really need both your arms working and the right arm he used to guide would fall away and he'd basically be running with one arm. So we'd be constantly saying, `Gerrard use your right arm as well as your left arm'. It becomes second nature in the end," Bruce says.

While the focus on technique is ongoing, the biggest improvements were made after the first year. Bruce also asked Gerrard to stop adding his own sessions. "He used to think running more would help him improve and I reckon he used to sneak sessions in. I caught him out a few times. He's learnt to trust me a lot more. You need your faith in your coach. You shouldn't be questioning him. As a result he's just been running quicker and quicker," Bruce says.

Gerrard ran a PB of 4:21 in the first round of the 1500m at the Beijing Games and finished sixth in 4:24.65. His rivals in the 1500m were in their 20s, an age when Gerrard was running ultras. "It is a tremendous achievement for a 38-year-old to PB at a major championship and to make a final," Robbie says, adding that the excessive noise generated by major crowds tends to over-stimulate blind athletes.

Gerrard has used his drive to challenge himself, such as by his goal to climb Mt Everest and his five-time feat of running 2000km (his PB is 13 days), to inspire and motivate others. "I have a very simple philosophy and that is if you think you're too small to be effective then you haven't been bitten by a mosquito. One person can make a difference. I've seen a lot of people who have had their heartbreaks in life and they have died at the age of 50 and they are buried at the age of 80. And what I mean by that is that their whole window of attitude is choked up with the disappointments, the heartbreaks, and that's where they lose sight of the big picture," Gerrard says.

"Thirty years of their life is just spent doing seriously nothing at all. That's why they need to take out the squeegee and wipe it away and make sure they have a clear focus. You could be absolutely frustrated out of your mind because you're totally blind you can't find something or a guide runner hasn't turned up or is injured. Success is a journey never a destination. It doesn't stop whether it's completing high school, university or a job - you always look at that next challenge to pursue," Gerrard says.

Gerrard says he has since received invitations to race in four marathons: Singapore, Nairobi, Mumbai and Hong Kong.

"That was unheard of five years ago: to have blind athletes invited, all expenses paid, to these events. That's because of the awareness and the appreciation of efforts and their abilities has really come through," Gerrard says.

His next key goal is representing Australia at the 2012 London Paralympics again. Training for Gerrard consists of daily runs, one-hour stretching sessions four times a week and three swims a week. He gets up at 4:30am to complete his training. He also does a lot of visualisation to prepare for races. "I don't train and visualise the track. What I try to do is feel the race, how the rope is going to feel in my hand. If I am running well, the rope is going to feel eased and relaxed in my hand. If I am struggling, then the rope is going to feel pretty taught and tight because my guide runner is in front of me, or not in front of me but pulling on it pretty hard. Or if I am feeling really fresh and I am out in front and pulling the guide runner along. You try to visualise how the rope is going to feel in the hand, how your breathing is going to sound when you're running well, all those sort of things," he says.

Despite the extra hurdles he has to overcome, Gerrard says in the end every runner has to battle that same opponent. "The thing about distance running is that many times you're actually competing against yourself."

(First published in Run For Your Life in 2008)

CHAPTER 3

As Gerrard Gosens, who was born blind, approached the finish line of the 10km held at the annual Melbourne Marathon he asked his guide runner how many competitors were in front of him. One, was the answer. "And I said, `What about the rest of them?' and he said, `They are all behind us'," says Gerrard, who went on to finish second overall. Gerrard still regards that moment as the highlight of his impressive running career. "Not only to come second but to actually beat all those other thousands of people who were able-bodied athletes."

While running is an individual sport, it is definitely a team effort for visually impaired athletes like Gerrard Gosens. They need guide runners for every training run and each race. Gerrard has a team of up to twelve guide runners and his wife Heather also often will guide him riding her bike. Finding, training and managing his team of guide runners requires work.

"It's an ever-evolving team because you have guys who will get injured, who will come and go, who will have a rest from the sport. And you are always training and coaching guys because not every person can guide a person who is blind. Some people have the ability to do it and some don't," Gerrard says.

For an elite distance runner like Gerrard, the pool of guide runners is limited because of the speed required to keep up with him relatively comfortably and leave enough energy to guide him as well.

"You do need to be a lot quicker," says Bruce Jones, who has been one of Gerrard's guide runners for the past seven years and became his coach as well four years ago. He estimates that a guide runner should be able to run at least 10 seconds per kilometre faster than the runner they are guiding. Of course the faster – and more elite - the visually impaired runner, the harder it is to find a suitable guide. "If he was running 3:00 per kilometre, you'd have to be able to run 2:50 or 2:45," Bruce says.

Bruce no longer runs competitively at elite level and has found it increasingly tough to guide Gerrard in his speed sessions or races. "I've had a few injury problems over the last year so it has been a struggle for me to be able to do the sessions and to even guide Gerrard in a race. Whereas years ago I could be really unfit and still at Gerrard's pace easily run and talk to him. You could be running along the road and there could be a low tree branch dangling down, so you have to really be alert and say, `Gerrard duck now', or you got to tilt him the other way. If I was tired and struggling sure enough he would run into a post that I have accidentally led him into. Not everyone can do it. There are elite runners that actually can't guide, they just don't have that knack," Bruce says.

Gerrard ran his first marathon and ultramarathon when he was a teenager, which he did mainly because that was what his guide runners did. But at the Beijing Paralympics in 2008 he ran the 1500m at the age of 38 just because he could. "I suppose the unusual thing for me is that most runners start short distances at a very young age and work their way up to ultra-marathons. I've done the opposite. I've gone from running ultra-marathons down to the very short distances. It's like when you are around the bush and you are camping. If you're trying to cook a meal for yourself you work with the resources that you actually have," Gerrard says.

With a rising profile over two decades of running and the help of Bruce he's been able to find more and faster guide runners to run with him. Dennis Fitzgerald is the most elite guide in his team and led him in Beijing. "I probably have only three or four that I would use in a race. I have one very elite one which obviously I took to Beijing. Like with a motorcar, you have your tires that are for racing and you have those ones that are for qualifying," Gerrard says.

To be sure, Gerrard brought other potential guide runners with him to Beijing, just in case his No. 1 guide, Dennis, would get injured or sick. "We had at least four people in that squad in Beijing so that if that first guide runner was to injure himself, we'd have other people who could run as well. It was good that Australia could spend the money on having some reserves over there," Bruce says.

As awareness and publicity for Paralympic athletes have soared after the Games in Sydney, Athens and Beijing, so has the availability of resources for athletes with a disability, says Robbie Bolton, national distance coach for the Paralympic Committee.

"The TV coverage has been more significant for each Games basically since Sydney. I think the public awareness generally has been raised more significantly each time. Gerrard has got quite a high profile in Brisbane and a lot of people know of him when he races and is doing his trials and his training. That's probably helped him in a number of areas. Some of these topics move into each other in terms of awareness and opportunities for distance runners. For him in particular it does require very much a team approach and it's quite a considerable effort to bring that together and that's a big strength that Gerrard has. He has quite a few members of his team, not only the guide runners and his coach, but his family and other guide runners that help him out locally in Brisbane as well as sports psychologists, nutritionists and physiologists. So it becomes quite a big management exercise to coordinate that on his part. As a result of the increased exposure I suppose, more people have been willing to come forward and help him out in that regard," Robbie says.

Besides a need for speed, the best guide runners for the tall Gerrard have been those that match his height, Robbie says. "The fascinating thing with Gerrard is that really I've come to the conclusion that physical size actually matters. It's very important that Gerrard is in sync with his guide runner. Gerrard is actually quite a tall man. From what I can see, the best guide runners with Gerrard have been the ones that have matched his physical characteristics. Shoulder height, for instance, with his direct guide runner is almost exactly the same and their stride is almost exactly the same in length. So it's a bit of a matching exercise with the guide runners. And they do a lot of training together as well to make sure that that happens," says Robbie.

When Gerrard is racing with Dennis, they are linked by a very short rope, Bruce says. That's possible because their heights are similar and it provides the control needed in a short race like the 1500m. Bruce says guiding an elite runner on the track is much more complicated than in, say, a marathon. "It'd be definitely harder in a 1500m race because it's a lot more to do with technique. If Gerrard's running with his No. 1 guide runner he has to use the real short rope because it gives you the ultimate control any time anyone sort of has a bit of a fall in the race, or you need to pass someone. With the marathon, technique is not as imperative. You just got to be relaxed. The guide runner could use a longer rope basically because you don't have any of the sudden movements where you have to stop him suddenly," Bruce says.

If Bruce, who is shorter than Gerrard, guides him they use a longer rope. "Or else my arms would be a lot higher or

Gerrard's arm would be a lot lower to get the swing going when you actually run and your arm goes forward," Bruce says.

Gerrard encourages people to volunteer as guide runners. He says that visually impaired athletes might be hesitant to seek out guide runners, while at the same time potential guide runners might not know how to be proactive. "There is always a need for more guide runners and that is where that void begins. If you have the guide runners, the people who are blind or visually impaired will have the confidence to say, `I can go and do this because I can find a guide runner'. Right now there's that gap between the confidence of stepping out and saying, I need a guide runner. It's a bit of both worlds. You've got the people who are saying, `Shall I ask if he actually wants to run?' and the blind people thinking, `Should I actually go and see if they are available to run with me'."

It is a similar story when it comes to entering races. Robbie says that most race organisers will be accommodating to disabled runners. He says often it is a matter of making race organisers aware that a runner with special needs would like to participate and specify what those needs are. "If people at the local level are going to compete and are going to participate then if they let the organisers know, then generally I have found that the organisers to be more than willing to help to the best of their ability," Robbie says.

Gerrard encourages any runners willing to guide another to contact him. He says that being relaxed is important when guiding a visually impaired runner. "When you are holding a guide rope and for example when I am holding a person's elbow, it is like riding a horse. When you are riding a horse, you don't keep the reins tight on the horse. You keep them relaxed so you can feel how the horse is moving. If you keep your arms stiff and the rope stiff while you're running, then I can't feel what's happening with your body," Gerrard says.

Of course communication between the two athletes is crucial, though the level depends very much on the race situation. "Whether you're running on the road or on the track, there are different levels of communication. In a 1500m there's not a lot of time for a lot of communication because it is a very tactical race. In the Beijing race there was a lot of toss and tumble, there was a lot of argy bargy in the sense of elbowing and the tactical stuff. In a 5km, 10km or a marathon, you have a lot of time to talk about where the other guide runners are," Gerrard says.

A visually impaired runner puts a lot of trust into the guide runner. Guides and their athletes will typically spend a lot of time together on regular training runs as well as in races. It certainly helps if you get along well, Bruce says. "I don't think it would work if you clashed with your guide runner. You've got to be a good friend as well to put up with all the things that could go wrong. A lot of times on easy runs you are talking and you need the same interests. We've been away an awful long time together. Ten weeks I've actually been away with Gerrard as well as with the other guide runner, Dennis."

Sometimes, Gerrard says, the most difficult part is near the finish line. "The really tricky thing is getting used to guide runners' estimates of distances. You might be running with a guide runner in a 10km and they'll say, `There's 500m to go,' and a kilometre later you're still running. Or you can be coming close to a finish and they'll say, `There's 400m to go,' and in 10m you cross the line. You're obviously trying to kick down and run faster for the end of a race, you're trying to use up every ounce of energy you have left. What is 1km to one person is very different to the next person. Estimates can be way out."

CHAPTER 4

Shelley Maxwell-Smith did her first triathlon in February at the fifth annual TriShave All-Women's Festival near Sydney. "I definitely thought the event would be less intimidating without blokes in the mix. I thought this would be relatively low key and non-competitive. It has a reputation for having a lot of first timers involved, which I was too," Shelley says.

That's exactly what Nick Munting, race director for Triathlon New South Wales in Australia and X-Tri Australia, wants to hear. The introduction of all-women's races has helped boost TriNSW's female membership to about 25 percent in 2007. That's an increase from the 20 percent it was for 15 of the previous 18 years in which Nick has been involved in the sport. While Nick is happy with the increase, he'd like to see more: "Promotion of women's sport is a definitive core focus activity for TriNSW."

Nationwide, women account for about 30 percent of Triathlon Australia's members. The struggle to attract more women isn't just an Australian issue. According to International Triathlon Union media manager Stephen Bourdeau, women account for about 10 percent of the triathletes in Japan, compared with about 30 percent in the US and about 40 percent in Canada. Most national federations don't track athletes based on gender, Stephen says. "We can't give accurate figures."

While triathlon can be both a costly and time-consuming sport, it is also an individual one that offers participants satisfaction regardless of experience, ability, age – and gender. That provides a simple target. "The goal is to lift women's participation through the sport to 50 percent," Nick says.

And as far as Nick is concerned, women-only events are the answer. "Beyond all other measures put in place in the last two decades, the all-women's event signifies a great - if not the singular best - way for women to experience the sport itself through dedicated events, with no gender pressure, and in a safe environment of total participation and minimum competition," he says.

Shelley agrees. "The women-only events are successful because women are still a bit intimidated by men in the field. I've heard stories about being bashed around in the swim and although girls are quite capable of this, I think the whole atmosphere is just more competitive when you add testosterone into the mix. My experience in the women's event was that everyone was very courteous and supportive of one another. There may have been some competitive tension at the front of the field but for the majority it was a largely non-competitive atmosphere."

While the absence of men makes the sport more appealing to some women, there are many other reasons why gender-equal fields in mixed triathlons are still quite a way off - especially as the race distance increases.

In the 2007/2008 Australian summer's sprint events at Kurnell, south of Sydney, female entries accounted for about 29 percent of the field, Nick says. At the Olympic level, Nowra had a 37.7 percent rate, Newcastle 27.2 per cent and Cronulla 19.9 percent most recently. At the 2007 Capricorn Half Ironman, there was a 25.6 percent female rate. And while more women are tackling Ironman races in Australia, they represented just 19.7 percent of the field at Western Australia in 2007. That is up from 9 percent at Ironman Western Australia in 1995.

Sam Bellgardt entered the sport a year ago when her personal trainer suggested she do a triathlon as part of a team. Sam was to do the 3-kilometre run, while two others would do the 300-metre swim and the 13-kilometre cycle. "I think the unfortunate thing about triathlon is that for the uninitiated it can look incredibly daunting. I'd really never considered it before it was suggested by someone else and I probably would never have thought of it on my own," says Sam who agreed to become part of the gym's team. "I was quite excited at the prospect."

So excited that when the gym team was cancelled days later Sam signed up to do the entire event herself. "It was really the fact that someone else thought I might be able to do it that made me start to believe that maybe I actually could. I decided that as I was interested in it, there was nothing to stop me from having a go on my own. Another friend who rides a lot then helped me find a suitable road bike and three months later I was at the starting line," Sam says.

She finished that triathlon and loved it. Sam is racing several triathlons this year including Noosa and the Bribie Triathlon series. She has joined a triathlon squad and trains with it whenever she can as she must coordinate her training with her husband's for his first marathon.

Completing a triathlon made Sam realise she had a lot in common with most other female and male competitors. "Until I actually became involved, I was quite frightened that I wouldn't be good enough or fast enough to be anything more than an impediment on a triathlon course. Then I began to realise that a very small percentage of the field is fighting out for the big prizes. Everyone else is pretty much just like me. Your biggest competition is yourself and the time you set last time you raced the distance, and coming across the finish line is an achievement in itself. No one laughs at you if you come in near the end of the field. They just keep cheering you on because you made it across the line," Sam says.

Tess Waterhouse is a seasoned competitor at Half Ironman and Ironman distances. She usually finishes at or near the top of her age group, and has raced in at the Ironman World Championships in Hawaii twice. Tess became a mum in April 2007 and returned to the sport soon after.

"Age group women, I think, definitely face more challenges than the males as often a household relies very heavily on the female: cooking, cleaning, shopping, communicating, scheduling of events, nurturing, paying bills etc, as well as go to work. This is certainly the case with me and even though Mal is one of the most supportive husbands around, things fall apart very quickly if I am not there. Females are more self-sacrificing than males in general and therefore it's harder to find the time to train, keep the house and the household together," Tess says.

While training and racing after becoming a parent hasn't always been easy, the benefits far outweigh the negatives for her and her family. "I started training two months after the birth of [son] Ben as I enjoy the challenges it throws but it is not easy balancing work, family and training. Many thought I was crazy to set such a goal, especially my coach Tim A'hern, so soon after the birth of Ben. Sometimes the balance isn't there and something has to give but I certainly believe it makes me a better parent as I am happy with myself as I feel fit, self confident and have an interest that allows me to meet some great people," says Tess.

Sam agrees. She says it is all about being organised. She and husband Tom have a finely balanced training schedule that fits with their hectic information technology jobs and looking after three-year-old son Luka. "My husband and I work in the IT industry on a 12-hour shift basis. We are extremely supportive of each other and our training needs. You just have to be extremely organised weeks in advance with what training you're doing, and completely diligent about doing the training that you've set yourself at the allotted time," Sam says.

Besides a reluctance to make time for themselves, women can also be more conscious than men about the family budget, says triathlete Liz Swinton. "If you are serious about competing, triathlon can be a costly sport to enter and many women are loath to spend money on themselves when the needs of a family can be seen to be more pressing. Setting yourself up for three sports, let alone club membership and race entry fees, is not an inexpensive exercise. In saying that, the weekend warrior-type triathletes can get by comfortably with a hybrid bike, a pair of runners and some swimmers," says Liz.

Liz is in her third season as a triathlete. It all started at a wedding. "I was in Noosa to attend a wedding - mine in fact - at the same time as the Noosa Triathlon. I was inspired by the athletes and the event to have a go at the sport. At the time I had forgotten that the only swimming I had completed was a personalised form of breaststroke that did not get my hair wet and was usually prompted by a cold glass of Chardonnay at the end of an eight-metre pool."

As a business owner, Liz also has to make the most of the time she can set aside to train. So she immediately enlisted the help of a coach. She is on a Rod Cedaro training program. "I am a time-poor person and I believe in having experts do the job they are qualified for. I have a mechanic fix my car, a plumber take care of any tap leaks etc and I feel that a triathlon coach is more than value for money. I don't consider having a coach devise a training program as a luxury; I consider it a necessity to get the most out of my limited ability, knowledge and time. I cycle with triathlon and cycling friends when my training program and time allows. My training partner is my husband and we do the majority of our running, swimming and biking together or with friends."

Liz's main goal this year is the Mooloolaba tri, which she has done twice before, the Gatorade series and possibly her first half Ironman.

Zoe King says that women can be harder on themselves than men, preventing some from even trying the sport. "The perception from sporty women who don't do triathlon that it is too hard training for all three disciplines and you have to be really good at all three. The men accept more willingly that they will be weaker at one discipline. Also there are some body-image pressures with women in that they don't want to become too bulky or lose their female shape," says Zoe, who did her first triathlon five years ago. "My previous company entered the BRW Triathlon in Sydney so I decided to have a go with some colleagues."

Since then Zoe moved up in distance from sprint triathlons to finishing her first Ironman last year. "It was such a buzz at the first race that I kept going. I like the variety of training for three sports rather than just one. Running is my favourite because it feels the most natural but I enjoy the challenge of combining all three in one race. The distances have increased over the last two years as I wanted to push my fitness level upwards. I found that I preferred the longer distance," says Zoe. She says she feels more competitive at the half Ironman distance. "Also the training load is manageable with my work and social lifestyle. Ironman definitely takes more sacrifices which is fine if you can do it at that time. Half Ironman fits in better with my lifestyle."

Women-only events don't appeal to Zoe. "I found the level was really catering for beginners hence not as competitive so I wouldn't do it again. I prefer mixed anyway as a better atmosphere - I like the competitiveness and I think the testosterone effect of the men does add excitement in the race."

Other reasons cited for female triathletes being a minority include that poor body image results in a lack of self-confidence to participate in sport; that triathlete role models especially the women such as Michellie Jones and Emma Snowsill don't get enough general media coverage; the fact that female triathlon coaches are a rarity; and personal safety running as well as road safety for cyclists.

TriNSW's Nick Munting says triathlon is certainly not male-oriented. "In fact triathlon flies in the face of what many of the males want most times. It stays dedicatedly gender fair – for instance prize money remains equal despite a small percentage of elite women competing alongside big numbers of elite males in many events. Most - all TriNSW and X-tri - events allow women to compete in dedicated waves, together with additional time buffers to the next male swimmers, to allow the ladies an uninterrupted swim. And so on. There's no fair call in saying the sport is male-oriented, other than saying the larger percentage of the sport's athletes remains male at this time," says Nick.

Being a minority doesn't mean that female triathletes face less rivalry, says Tess. "There are certainly less competitors than for the males. But if you think about it, a woman never crosses the line first and rarely last so the time that women finish in is actually less of a range, i.e. in Ironman from 9 to 17 hours, as opposed to males, 8 to 17 hours. Certainly in the longer races there is fantastic competition among the females and many a male has been humbled as a female passes them in the run."

Every triathlete remembers their first race and most – if not all – would have felt intimidated for one reason or another. That's probably one of the reasons that most triathletes, male and female, are an encouraging bunch. So the biggest hurdle is to get women to try their first triathlon.

Often, once that first hurdle is passed, a new level of confidence and a new passion are found. "Most women are moving on from the women-only events quite quickly," Nick says. Three women who did their first triathlon this year's TriShave All Women's race went on to compete in the Kurnell Sprint race a week later, he says.

Since her women-only introduction to the sport, Shelley has joined Sydney Triathlon Group (STG) and raced in the NSW Club Championship in May – guys allowed.

"STG has been absolutely fantastic in building both my fitness and my confidence. Training with guys is really beneficial to racing with them too. I've found the coaches and the other members at STG - male and female - really encouraging. And although a lot of them are really competitive athletes, they've still got time to shout encouragement or even stick with you in an ocean swim. I think being part of a triathlon group breaks down any potential intimidation women may feel by the guys who, in my experience, have been nothing but great," Shelley says.

(First published in Australian Triathlete in 2008)

CHAPTER 5

Runners tend to be determined people, and for better or worse, follow their hearts. Often it turns out for the better and in Ron Stuart's case it made him an age group world champion. In 1993 Ron, who is now 75, was training for his first appearance at the World Masters Athletics Championships in Miyazaki, Japan. He told his coach, Stan Johnston, that he had entered the 2000m steeplechase, 5000m, 10,000m and the 8km cross country events.

"Stan looked at me very seriously and said, 'At your age and if you wanted to continue running, do you think it is a good idea to do the steeple? If I was you, I'd pull out of the steeple'. I said, 'Oh well righto, if that's what you think I should do'."

On his way to Japan, Ron won his age group in a 5000m race in Hong Kong in about 19:02, also beating the people in the age group below his. In Japan, he faced some world champions in the 5000m, 10,000m and the cross country. "I wasn't too good in that," Ron says.

"I hadn't run in the main oval [for any of those events] so I thought I'd like to do that and the steeple was on the last day in the main stadium. Having done no specified training for the steeple, I went over the night before and I found I could get over the steeples. I didn't try the water jump. I thought, well I can remember how that was done. I thought I'll go in the steeple and I won't tell Stan."

Ron won the 2000m steeple in 7:51:96, setting an Australian 60+ age record. "When I came back home, I had to confess to Stan that much against his wishes I'd run the steeple. It just shows the standard wasn't very good if without specific training I could just do that."

Ron's running career started several decades earlier, when he won a scholarship to Scotch College in Melbourne. Each student had to run every athletic event and won points if they passed certain standards.

"If you got the A-grade standard, you got 2 points and you were also automatically included in the training squad for the school athletic team. I was hopeless at the 100m. I tried to duck the two judges at the end. They'd stand and then bring the rope down to stop anyone who was over time. Even though I was short I was unable to get under the rope. So I missed the 100m and the 200m. A couple of times I made the 440m. I certainly could get the 880m and I romped in the mile. I passed the A-grade standard and I was in the school athletic team. I ran with the Old Boys and for about five years I was unbeaten in cross country over a range of distances from about 3 miles to about 10."

Ron trained and raced with a who's who of Australian running. He was coached by Percy Cerutty as were John Landy, Merv Lincoln and Dave Stephens. "I'd beat Merv Lincoln in the university 3-mile state championship. I used to beat Dave

Stephens, the Flying Milko, until he went and stayed six months with Emil Zatopek," Ron says.

Ron credits Percy with teaching him to run properly and to train to the best of his ability. "For example, he would sometimes have us running around the park trying to be like butterflies. The idea was to flit over the ground just touching down momentarily, not hitting the ground like a draught horse and then pushing off again. His training methods were well in advance of anyone else at that time and I learnt much from him - I don't get the injuries that many of my younger friends get."

Percy demanded a lot of his athletes as Ron experienced first-hand. "He pushed us hard. I fell down the stairs at work one time and hurt my leg enough to think of missing training that night. However I went to tell him what happened and he said, 'You broke your leg did you?' I said, 'No.' He then said that I should only do 14 repetition 440s at 70 sec instead of the 20 reps he had set," Ron says.

Ron studied accounting but Percy wanted him to focus on running. "He set goals for everyone and if he thought you were not giving it everything you had then he lost interest in you. When he wanted me to stop doing my part-time university course so that I could train more intensively to become a world champion, I refused as I said I could not live by just running. If you won a prize worth the equivalent of $5 in those days you

48

were disqualified for life from all competition as a professional. He then asked me to train with someone else. And John Landy had the same problem with Perce. He was starting with university and Perce wanted him to stop and he said no, so Percy told Landy to go too."

While selected for the training squad preparing for the 1956 Olympics in Melbourne, Ron hurt his leg in training and didn't make the team. He then contracted polio in 1958 which ended his early running ambitions. Ron joined Commonwealth Bank of Australia (CBA) as a letter boy and after graduating in the late 1950s, he moved to the bank's economic department. Ron married Ruth in 1960. That same year CBA was split into Commonwealth Banking Corporation and Reserve Bank of Australia (RBA) and Ron was transferred to the RBA in Sydney.

The Stuarts didn't know Sydney and Ruth looked at more than 400 houses before they chose one in Mosman, disregarding their agent's advice that that was a dreadful suburb. In 1965 the RBA transferred Ron to Papua New Guinea where they stayed five years.

Then Ron was interviewed by the International Monetary Fund, which seconded him to Swaziland in 1978. So the family moved to the kingdom bordered by South Africa and Mozambique. After they returned to Australia four years later, Ruth was diagnosed with breast cancer. The IMF asked Ron whether they'd be willing to go to The Gambia in West Africa. "Despite my wife's tenuous health she said, 'Yes, yes, let's go.' So we went. I was to assist in floating the currency and rescheduling the national debt which we were successful in doing." As Ruth's health deteriorated they went back to Sydney. "I'd retired at this stage to look after her at home. After she died [in mid-1991] I found that I was getting puffed putting my slip-on shoes on."

Ron's daughter Natasha tried to convince him to join a gym. She was very persistent and finally Ron relented. He took circuit classes led by Tani Ruckle, silver medallist for Australia at the Auckland Commonwealth Games in 1990. That's when he met Stan Johnston who took him on runs and became his running coach.

Soon Ron began winning his age group in fun runs and he went to the National Veterans Athletics Championships in Adelaide where he competed in the 5000m and 10,000m. One of the competitors in the race was Ron Young from Victoria. The two Rons had competed against each other in the early 50s.

"He ran for St Stephens and I ran for Old Scotch - mostly 3000m steeplechase and 3 mile races. He told me to keep running and we could have a good competition the next year. So with Stan's help I trained hard and we raced the next year in Sydney when I did 18:35 for the 5000m. I don't think Ron [Young] ran the 2000 steeplechase which I won in 7:58."

The increase in training also helped the then 63-year-old Ron win his age group in the Sydney Morning Herald half marathon in 84:54. "Since that time we have run against each other at the nationals and we enjoy it immensely. I was really tired in an 8km cross country in Sydney that year and I had been running just behind Ron for the first 4km - we had to run two laps - and I was thinking that I was too tired to do another lap and might pull out.

"However I noticed he was also struggling so I made an effort and ran past him quickly for some 100m and then dropped back to my previous pace. I ended up beating him by about 150m. It shows how you can talk yourself into or out of doing well."

Ron says it is important to focus during races. "I am thinking of all the things I have to do. I find that you are thinking about your pace, about your style, whether you are relaxed, how your shoulders are, what your neck is like, are you lifting your knees, are you kicking up too high at the back, where are your competitors, how you can catch them up or how you can get further in front and you want to be watching all the time how fast you are going because if you get sucked up in the start and go too quickly that can ruin your race at the end. Then you are thinking about where you are in your training and whether it is where you want it to be."

Ron's preparations for the 1997 world championships in Durban, South Africa, were going well until he broke his leg three days before he was due to leave. With his leg in plaster, Ron talked with his doctor and says it went something like this:

Doc: "You are not going to the games now."

Ron: "What are you going to do if I stay?"

Doc: "Well nothing really."

Ron: "Well I am going."

"So I went and Harry Gathercole, the Australian 93-year old sprinter, saw me on the plane just as we were getting off and said, 'You silly young bugger, can't you look after yourself?' So age is just relative."

After the championships Ron met his daughter Natasha and went back to Swaziland, followed by a safari in Botswana. "I'd had to send a medical certificate to say that I was fit and capable of doing this. When I broke my leg I thought, 'I won't send them another medical certificate.' When we finally got off the plane, the leader's mouth just dropped when he saw me getting off the plane with crutches. He said, 'we are going for a big walk this afternoon.' I said, 'that's all right I'll be there.' So we walked about eight miles that afternoon and I made sure I was behind the leader at all times."

The next world championships were held in the UK in 1999. "By this time I'd woken up that this was a good excuse to go

52

for a holiday. So after the games I set off by myself and went to St Petersburg and caught the Siberian-Mongolian railway to Beijing which took me a month. I kept on getting off. I got off at Ulan Bator and stayed in a yurt, went riding. I like the Mongolian horses, they are more my size - a bit smaller and very powerful. I ended up in Beijing, had a look at the Great Wall and so forth, and the Forbidden City."

Ron then spent two weeks in South Korea. After the Puerto Rican championships, Ron visited Panama and Costa Rica while San Sebastian was a great base to explore Morocco, by camel. He has also seen Greenland via dogsled, hiked to Machu Picchu in Peru, cycled in Cambodia and took the "soft" option to see Antarctica as it involved daily showers and a real bed.

Ron had run several marathons in his 20s. He finished his first in less than 3 hours and his fastest in about 2:30. One race stands out clearly in his memory. Within sight of the finish, Ron sat down in the gutter and started taking his shoes off when his father helped him change his mind with "a few choice words".

When Ron resumed running more than 30 years later, he "vowed and declared" never to do another marathon. But with some help of Susan Griffith, coach of the Northside Running Group of which Ron is a member, word spread that Ron was planning to do the 45-kilometre off-road Six Foot Track in 2004. "Much against my better judgement I started training for it."

Ron researched the course and did several long runs in the Blue Mountains. He would be 71 on race day and no one over the age of 70 had finished the hilly trail race within the 7-hour cut-off time. Ron, two others in their 70s and three in their 60s were allowed to start an hour early. Ron got to Cox's River (at 15.5km) 3 minutes ahead of his schedule and went past Pluviometer (at 26km) 25 minutes ahead of plan. He finished in 6:48:31, the first and only person over 70 that year to make the cut-off.

Ron has just entered a new age group in turning 75. His training was interrupted in April and May by two cataract operations and he had to skip the most recent Sydney Morning Herald half marathon. His main goal now is the world championships in September in Riccione, Italy.

"I couldn't have had it [the layoff] at a worse time. I find that the older you get, the quicker you lose your fitness and that it takes about three times as long as when you were young to get it back again. I don't give myself much chance of getting back to a competitive edge but I'll give it a go - I have got nothing else to do," Ron says, laughing.

His post-race travel plans include Turkey and Egypt.

Ron trains as many as seven days a week and runs twice on Tuesdays and Thursdays. "I'd heard a couple of young ladies during a run say they were stopping because they couldn't keep up so I said, 'Right don't stop and keep running, come with me and we'll run together on a Tuesday and I'll run at your pace.' That became a fixture," he says.

In his 20s Ron also encouraged others. The Scotch College Great Scot newsletter quotes a letter from former Governor-General Peter Hollingworth who recalls that, at the personal encouragement throughout the 3000m steeplechase by team mate Ron Stuart, he ran a personal best by about 17 seconds to enable the club to go up to A-grade. Ron says, "Peter was kind enough to suggest that I had helped him a little - but when the last water jump approached I had to make sure that I finished first and I set off with about 150m to go. I think the St Kevin's runner splashed Peter rather badly and that made him cranky enough to really make sure he came second to me."

Ron still does one of Percy's sessions which is also one of his favourites. "Thursday I run at the oval in the morning and do repetition 400m. Five and upwards, depending of where I am in my training schedule. Just keep on doing 10 or 15 laps, alternating fast and slow," Ron says.

Another favourite is Monday's NRG session which until recently was organised by coach Susan. His training partners include the speedy 12-year-old twins Vida and Ziggy Robinson.

"Being with the others keeps me honest. I have got to push myself except when I really decide I am not going to punish myself," says Ron.

On Tuesday Ron runs 10 repetitions of 100m as fast as he can, which is about 18seconds. He also does easy runs on Thursday, Saturday and Sunday and goes to the gym on Wednesday and Friday. "I look at Vida sometimes and I think I can almost remember when I used to run like that. I find it difficult to believe that I was running that fast. I don't think about the past very often but it has been fun to think of the happy times long ago. I have been very fortunate."

Ron's training schedule

Monday:	NRG training (speed work or hill repeats)
Tuesday:	Morning: 10 x 100m in about 18 sec
	Evening: easy hour
Wednesday:	gym: spin class, weights, rowing
Thursday:	Morning: 400m reps (five or more)
	Evening: hour easy run
Friday:	gym: spin class, weights, rowing
Saturday:	80 min run with NRG
Sunday:	60 min run with Mosman gym group

(First published in Run For Your Life in 2007)

CHAPTER 6

Tony McClement knows his competitors well. The Sydney-based triathlete can tell you their best Ironman times as well as their top swim, bike and run splits. He knows their strengths and weaknesses, and whether or how often they've raced at the Ironman World Championships in Kona, Hawaii. If McClement doesn't know this information off the top of his head, he scans the spreadsheet he's created on the top guys in his 30-34 age group.

"I use the information to plan my race and mentally prepare myself for any possible outcomes," Tony says.

Neither age nor race distance seem to make a difference in the search for a competitive edge. Olympic-distance triathlete Kenneth Lewis, who competes in the 60-64 age group, uses the internet too. While he says his research may make no difference to his results, "I cannot remember a time when it hurt. Information is always better."

If you are too busy training, then you need someone like Mia Ursini. While an Ironman finisher herself, she has helped run the numbers on the competition for her partner Joe Esposito. "It helps to give him an idea how hard he needs to push in each discipline," Mia says.

Today's triathletes have all the information at their fingertips through the internet. That was not the case 10 years ago. Tim A'hern, who was Australian Ironman champion in 1991 and 1992, retired from competitive racing in 1997 and is now a coach.

Tim says in that in the 1990s results of rivals were found in triathlon magazines and *The Daily Telegraph* newspaper in Australia which then published triathlon race results almost weekly. Another source of information was triathletes racing overseas who called home with results. "We had no access to the internet. Our access to our opposition's results was through triathlon magazines so you had a fair idea what people could do. But now people – athletes that I coach anyway – tend to know people's races, what their best times are, what their strengths are and aren't. It's quite strategic now the way some of the athletes race. It's actually been a real eye opener for me the last few years how much these guys know about their opposition," Tim says.

Tony did his first triathlon in 1990 at Nepean, Australia, after reading about the sport in a magazine a year earlier. He loved it. In 2002, he did his first Ironman in Penticton, Canada, followed by Ironman New Zealand in 2003, finishing in 10:50 and 10:49 respectively. Then he decided to stay closer to home and raced Ironman Australia in Forster-Tuncurry in 2004. He improved his time to 10:19 and decided to join a training squad coached by John Hill.

When Tony raced Ironman Australia in 2005, his consistent training and experience paid off, and he cut another 30 minutes off his time. Tony then knew that qualifying for Kona was within reach. So he signed up for Ironman Western Australia, held in

Busselton in November 2005, and followed the advice of his coach John. John told Tony that besides discipline in training and a solid race plan, he needed to know who else was racing. So Tony turned to the internet and Google. "With my ability improving and the chance of Hawaii a real possibility going into Busselton 2005, I wanted to see how many guys were actual threats and how many weren't," Tony says.

While Tony had another solid Ironman at Busselton, he just missed out on a Kona slot and set his sights on Ironman Malaysia 2006. This time Tony really did his homework. "I knew exactly what each athlete had done and where I should be in the race, and what I was required to do to achieve success. When I got out of the water, I was in third," as he expected. "When I moved into second about 20km into the ride, I wasn't surprised."

At the bike turnaround, Tony was 3 minutes down on the guy leading his age group. "I knew who he was, and knew that he was a strong swimmer, rode the same as me, but never had run faster than a 4-hour marathon. As far as I was concerned, as long as I didn't lose 30 minutes to him, I was going to beat him."

The end result though was far from decided. "Before the race, I knew there were at least seven threats. At the turn I saw that five were riding together about 5 minutes back. I knew that they were riders as strong as me, and could run within my time. The best rider, who was the weakest swimmer, was 25 minutes down and I knew he wasn't going to catch me without blowing up. At this point - knowing exactly where everyone was - I decided to re-evaluate my plan. Knowing I didn't have to worry about the one in front, I only had to worry about those behind me. I was questioning whether I should wait and ride with the other guys, or ride my own pace and let them catch me, minimising any loss to the leader. In the end I rode my own pace and let the guys catch me - as they didn't ride together, but solo, each trying to break each other. Getting off the bike I felt strong and saw that I was only a few minutes down on the leader and the riders behind had spent 180km chasing me, only to get within 1 minute of me."

While Tony says running a marathon is less about strategy, he didn't let his pace be dictated by the competitors he considered threats to his Kona slot. "At 20km [into the run] I was sixth, as all in front had sprinted the first 15km. By 30km I moved into second and held on. In the end, only two of us ran faster than 4 hours."

Tony had his ticket to the world championships in Kona.

Tony's account is an increasingly familiar one to triathlon coach Tim A'hern. "I've got guys who I coach who know exactly where they have got to finish in their age group, who is in their age group, where they think they can finish and if they think they will get a roll-down spot [for Kona]. It's quite amazing. They pretty much know the people and have a fair idea of whether those people would actually take the spot," Tim says.

The increased volume and speed of online information about races and the athletes also have helped Tim. "As a coach now, I have guys race and I pretty much know their results before they even call me. As long as the race organisers are on the ball they post the results pretty quickly. You see what people's splits are and when they are calling, I know exactly what they've done so I've had to time to have a look at it and have a think about it."

While Tim see some advantages to the increased flow of information, he encourages his athletes to focus on themselves.

"They can become too focused on what their competitors are doing. For instance on the bike if they catch up to Joe Bloggs who they know has finished Top 3 in their age group, some of them will not have confidence in their own ability. I teach them to have confidence in their own ability, go off a lot of pacing and how they feel. I like them to be able to pace themselves without worrying too much about who's around and what they are doing, and concentrate on their own race. I know there's a few of them who are really looking at who's around them and they go off that, which I am not real keen on. They should get in there and go as hard as they can. It is really important to be able to concentrate on your own race and how you feel, and not concentrate on what's going on around you," Tim says.

While Tim will not actively encourage his athletes to research their competitors, he sees no point in discouraging them from doing so either. "If they are going to come to me and ask me, they are going to do it anyway. Half the time they've already pretty much worked out that they want to find out who's in their age group and what's going on. Most know exactly who's in their age and how many guys are in their age, and how many spots there are, and where they already perceive themselves to be as far as that goes," Tim says.

And he has seen success with opposite approaches at Ironman Australia in Port Macquarie for two of his athletes, who became husband and wife two months earlier. "They had completely different strategies. She knows everybody in her age group and the guy wouldn't know who he was racing against. She ended up second in her age group and he ended up third in his," Tim says. Both qualified for Kona, and now their honeymoon includes the world championships in October. It already did, but they had planned on being spectators, Tim says.

Tony, who has raced nine Ironmans and has finished five of them under 10 hours, now has his research method down pat. "Once the entry is closed and the race list is printed usually one month out from race start, I download the category under the titles Race Number, Name, Country. From here I basically short-list the group into athletes who have finished in less than 10 hours," Tony says.

Next, Tony googles the athlete's name followed *by Ironman triathlon*. "This usually brings up their Ironman results as well as triathlon results. Common names require a little bit of searching which is where the country comes in. The result page usually has all their Ironman results on page one and enables me to quickly see if they are a threat. No threat, i.e. finishing times over 10 hours, are deleted and not thought about again. Those who have finished faster than 10 hours I tick for further research. If they are multi-finishers and have shown some improvement and are down to 10hours 30mins, I will mark them for further research. But it will depend on the final numbers that are threats."

Besides Google, Tony also uses the Yahoo search engine as well as My Space and Facebook to complete the picture - literally.

"These days most people have My Space or Facebook pages that show up and give photos, which enables me to get a mental picture of them - particularly when you get to the race and see them walking around. If they are a threat and looking fit, they are considered a threat. If they are looking chubby, no threat."

Then the real work begins. "Once I have my shortlist I research each athlete with a bit more effort. I actually pull up the athlete's best Ironman time. I record their overall time, as well as swim, bike, run splits and the course it was on. I also try to identify how the athlete performs under the upcoming race conditions, such as heat or hills. I analyse this information by determining their ability compared to mine. For example, what is their strength and where are they going to lose and make up time on me. I set my base-line performance as 55mins [for the swim], 5hrs 10mins [for the bike] and 3hrs 20mins [for the run]. How do they compare to that?" Tony says.

Like Tony, Joe Esposito also raced in Ironman Malaysia 2006, albeit in the 40-44 age group. It was the first race where this US triathlete researched his rivals. In fact his partner, Mia Ursini, gathered most of the information. "Malaysia was the first race we googled all the athletes because Joe's coach felt he had a strong chance to qualify for Kona since it was a small race. The previous year most of the competitors [at Malaysia] were able to get a slot to Kona, However, I think the secret got out. When I started looking up the guys in his age group, I got a little nervous for him," Mia says.

Joe's coach Peter Clode recommends researching rivals, especially when the goal is to qualify for Kona, Mia says. Since Malaysia 2006, she has looked up Joe's competitors online. "We check all the people in his age group, especially those with similar times. It usually will tell him how much time he needs to knock off to beat them," Mia says.

She and Joe look at splits for each discipline as well as transition times, and compare these to Joe's. "It helps to give him an idea how hard he needs to push in each discipline," Mia says.

Mia says she has a few friends who google their age group rivals before every race; she doesn't bother. "I'm much too slow to make it worth my effort. I love to have fun and keep a smile on my face the whole time. The one time I pushed myself when I got my new bike; I was racing against my own time," Mia says.

Joe has found that doing the research has created more pressure for him, and may work against him on race day. While much research is fuelled by the burning desire to secure that elusive Kona slot, Olympic distance triathletes such as Kenneth Lewis use it too. Kenneth grew up in Bondi Beach, Sydney, but now lives in the US. He's been a triathlete since 1982 and started researching his competitors about five years ago as he prepared for the ITU World Championships.

Kenneth says the number of competitors in his 60-64 age group is usually small enough to research them all. "I research for all major races and some minor races. First I check who is going to be in my race, if posted. Then I look if they've raced the same course in a prior year and I place their times in a spreadsheet. Then I check nationals and worlds to see if I have raced them in either of these prior races. If so, I log their times and mine for comparison. Also, I will google competitors I don't know. If I can find a race, then I see if there is someone in the same race for which I have data on.

"If my competitors are close to my times or better, then I log swim, bike, run and total times. If the competitor is a lot worse than me, then I just log their total time," he says.

Kenneth will analyse the splits of those competitors who have done similar race times to his own. "By looking at their splits I can tell where I should see them on the course. In some cases it may give me a strategy, i.e. keep him in sight on the bike course."

Kenneth says researching rivals is only useful for those athletes whose goal is to beat others, not for those athletes who prefer to focus on improving their times. "Most triathletes just go out there and try to improve their times or just try to finish. I race other competitors and don't really care about my times," he says.

Tony only does his research before Ironman races in which his primary goal is to qualify for Kona. And he stresses that no amount of research makes up for a lack of solid and consistent training. "When I want a race time, I focus on my race plan to get that time. When time doesn't matter, it is about place - then knowing who you are riding with is important. What I have learnt is that the research can only help you up to the end of the bike, as we know if you can't run, you won't qualify. In Australia if you can't run faster than 3:15, forget about Kona."

(First published in Australian Triathlete in 2008)

CHAPTER 7

.

Brian McCarthy is preparing for the 50-kilometre Ultra Bunbury Marathon in May, which will be his first ultra race. Less than a year ago he finished his first marathon in 3 hrs 54 mins. Not bad for a 42-year-old guy with two bad knees who got some not-so-subtle hints from his wife seven years ago, when he was smoking and about 16kg heavier, that it was time to get back into shape.

"I had progressed into a man who was probably going to scare the hell out of middle age. One birthday I came home and there's this big, huge weight collection in the shed. I got a gym set-up out the back that everyone would probably envy: three-odd weight benches, 280kg worth of weights, a chin-up and knee-up area, a couple of punching bags and stuff. Three to four people can work out at the same time without getting in each other's way," Brian says.

He took the hint and started using the weights. While he enjoyed it, he found it hard to keep his motivation consistent. He'd train regularly for about two months before "slacking off for six weeks", and then repeated the pattern. But it was a start.

Another nudge came from his job at a power station in Western Australia where he lives. His company participates in the annual Heart Foundation's Climb to the Top stair competition. "There is normally a group of 10 people and their ambition through the month with the whole group is to make it to the top of Mount Everest in terms of the amount of stairs that you climb or the amount of time that you train. I'd done that for a couple of years and in 2003 I actually won the WA title for the most amount of stairs climbed. I got myself a couple of vouchers out of that."

While that victory was an accomplishment, Brian was still smoking and approaching a milestone in September 2004.

"As my wife said, `You're turning 40'. That's all it was - you're turning 40."

So Brian started looking for a new goal. Two of his colleagues were planning to run the 2004 City to Surf in Perth. It got Brian thinking about his running days in the Navy, which he joined as a 17-year-old in 1982. Besides the Physical Training, part of the regular regime was a six-mile run every Wednesday afternoon. "Once a week we did what we used to call the shit-run. It was named that because you had to run past the sewerage works and then across some tidal mudflats. So first you had to run past the smell of the shit before ending up to your knees in it.

"I was lucky enough that two of the other guys that I shared a cabin with when I first did my training were really good runners. One of the guys used to win the run each week. He smoked a packet of Red Winfields a day, mind you, but we were 17, 18 so we were 10-foot tall and bullet proof. There was no structured distance running type program or anything like that. If you could run it, you ran it. If you got back first, you had plenty of spare time. I never made it into the top 10 [of that six-mile run] but I always gave it my best shot. That's probably how I got into the distance stuff because we'd do all the sprint events through school but I'd never touched on any distance," Brian says.

His run training remained haphazard until 1988 when he was based on the HMAS Swan with a few runners. "I got off the ciggies and the alcohol and got back running again. On the HMAS Swan there were couple of us into distance running. Whenever the ship was on shore we'd run alongside in the morning," Brian says.

He ran his first 10km race in November 1988. Shortly afterwards, following another transfer with the Navy and the loss of his running buddies, he started playing Aussie rules during which he seriously injured his right knee. That put his running ambitions on hold, especially when he severely strained his left knee playing indoor beach volleyball a couple years later. He didn't run again until he decided to join his colleagues in the 2004 City to Surf.

Given his 2003 victory in the Climb to the Top, Brian thought his fitness level was good, but during the race he changed his mind. "I realised exactly how unfit I was. The thing that really motivated me to stick with running] was on one of the last hills before the end of the course as you head into Perry Lakes. A chap who I imagined to be about 65 passed me going up the hill pushing his grandkid in a stroller and he was talking on the mobile phone at the same time. Now I was struggling to actually breathe and I just thought to myself, if this bloke can be doing this at 65, I'd just like to be able to make it up the hill when I am 65."

Brian finished the 12km race in 1 hour and 41 seconds. He stuck with his newfound motivation to resume a running regime and looked for ways to keep it. He found inspiration in John Bingham's *No Need for Speed: a Beginner's Guide to the Joy of Running*. He now also makes sure he has company because nothing is as motivating as knowing that somebody is waiting for you to show up. Brian's regular running buddy is 37-year-old Neil, who suffered brain injuries as a kid. "Neil enjoys running, and the friendships and the company he gets from it. I run with him quite regularly," Brian says.

Brian, one of his two sons and Neil signed up as members of the West Australian Marathon Club to join in their training runs and races. "There is always a run on the calendar that we can do so we always have something to strive for," Brian says. He ran five more races in 2004.

In 2005, he completed 20 races including the Fremantle Half Marathon, which he finished in 1 hr 51 mins. He also started a training log as recommended by Ray Boyd [a 2:13 marathon runner] in a seminar organised by the WA Marathon Club. "Ray couldn't emphasise enough the fact that the best thing you can ever do is to keep some sort of diary. He pulled about eight different exercise books and handed them around. He said, `Look you can put anything you like in there. It is up to but I recommend you put at least the time you are out, distance is not necessarily important, how you felt on the day and keep track of your shoes because normally after a while you end up with a few pairs'," Brian says.

And running shoes are definitely something Brian needs to keep track of. To protect his damaged knees he believes in rotating several pairs. "If I have to dodge and weave and put a lot of lateral stress on the knees, they tend to flare up. But just with the running and being pretty good with the training, I don't normally have too many problems with them. I take the fish oil tablets and the glucosamine to help keep things under control and help keep flare-ups down. As long as I don't overdo it and don't increase the mileage too much – which is what everyone tells you not to do but we all get a bit carried a way at times. And I rotate my shoes. I am the Imelda Marcos in my street of running shoes. I've got about 7 or 8 pairs on the go at any one time," he says.

Brian has two pairs each of the Brooks Beast, Asics Kayano and Asics Evolution models, and a pair of Nike Free shoes for beach runs. "I absolutely love running on the beach and I used to do that barefoot al the time but I had too many scares with broken bottles."

By 2006, his fitness level had improved to the point that Brian decided to sign up for the Perth marathon. He took advice from other members of the WA Marathon club and regularly ran in their races and training runs. The training paid off. "I was just over the moon. I couldn't have had a better day for a first marathon. I ran with a few friends for the first third of the event. Then I got pushed along by a couple of triathlete friends of mine who were doing the marathon and just managed to find that right rhythm to do the last 10km under my own steam and left every one else behind me. I had planned on a start/finish day and actually managed to get a sub-4 hour one. I was just rapt," he says.

While Brian is ecstatic with his time, he is often not that focused on his watch, partly to protect his knees. "I find if I focus too much on time, that's when I start to end up with some niggles. I had a good run the other year here in Mandurah. It was only a pretty small field and I actually got third across the line and then spent the next six weeks on the sideline with a blown calf so that was a wake-up call: let the rabbits go and enjoy the run. I don't like to be injured. I don't like to be sitting on the sideline like anyone else I suppose once they are pretty obsessed or committed to the cause," he says.

He also finds it more rewarding to chat to other runners during a race, particularly if that will help them through a tough spot. Brian has found a routine of running up to five days and 80km a week. He loves starting the day with a run. "Because I am a morning person I will very rarely run after work unless I have done a night shift. If I come off night shift, I will do a 10 or 12 km, come home and take the kids to school and then put myself to bed later. If I am working days or on my days off I can be up anywhere between 10 to 4[am] and 6[am] and go for a run. The work day just feels so much better after you have been for a run in the morning, it just cruises by. When I run by myself in the morning I enjoy that quality time alone."

Brian has found inspiration in many fellow runners, especially from some of the other members of the WA Marathon Club and now it is his turn to inspire others. When he sees an annual fun run in Rockingham missing from the calendar in 2006, he calls the organiser and offers to help. Within two days, his help is accepted and the run is successfully organised within six weeks. He is involved this year again, helping to get sponsors and being the master of ceremonies and commentator on the day. It looks like he is doing OK on the sponsorship front with a promise from Toyota for a car to be raffled among the event's entrants this year.

"What I like most about running is that anyone can do it. Now that I am quite fit and healthy, I can do quite a lot of things that I'd never have thought of doing before and hopefully I can still do it when I am 65."

Brian wants to help others make a similar transformation and support them to find an exercise routine until they enjoy it enough to keep it up. "It is easy to convert someone to be a runner

- they only need a pair of shoes. I don't mind going slow running, walking and all that sort of stuff to get people started. I am happy to work my training regime around anyone who is willing to get back into it," he says.

That includes his family. When one of his two sons took a year off from competitive ballroom dancing, Brian got him into running for a while - until he dragged him to a 5km race in Fremantle on an early Sunday morning when it was pouring rain and about 3 degrees. "After that he went, nah Dad nah," Brian says, adding that he expects his son to get back into running later.

Brian had also challenged his brother and sister to run the Melbourne Half Marathon with him in November this year. But with a ballroom dancing competition for his son scheduled on the Gold Coast in August, the goal has been changed to the Bridge to Brisbane run. Brian's sister had been running until she got injured after a race four years ago. "So I gave her the challenge, you get back into it and we'll run together."

Brian's brother works as a chef on an offshore gas field and has shed 18kg this year by running after Brian gave him a copy of Bingham's *No Need for Speed*. "At first he just pushed himself a bit too far, got shin splints and a bit down in the dumps because he couldn't get out there and do what he could do as when he was 21. Most of us do that when we get out again. And then he realised he could take it slow and steady. His eldest daughter has been out running and walking with him and motivating him as well so that is quite good," says Brian.

He now has his sights on widening his wife's athletic pursuits, which already include netball and volleyball. "I reckon I have just about got her converted. I reckon within a couple of months I might get her with a pair of running shoes on."

(First published in Run For Your Life in 2007)

CHAPTER 8

When Kate Rowe finished the Ironman World Championships 70.3 she thought she'd done OK. Then the 56-year-old Australian learnt she had become an age group world champion. "We went over to the results and I discovered that I'd actually won. I kid you not – I cried. It still hasn't sunk in really," Kate says.

She finished in 5:14:33, 10 minutes ahead of No. 2, age-group legend Missy LeStrange. Kate's 2:31:58 bike and 1:51:24 run were the 55-59 age group's fastest. It was an unexpected crowning of a tough journey in the world of triathlon that almost ended a year earlier. A doctor had pulled Kate out of Ironman Western Australia in November 2006 when she couldn't walk straight 10 kilometres into the run. She had hoped to qualify at WA for the Ironman World Championships in Kailua-Kona, Hawaii. Instead she got her first Did Not Finish (DNF). "I was truly devastated and I said, That's it. I am not doing this any more," Kate says.

Mentally, physically and financially exhausted from her third Ironman in 18 months, she believed the pinnacle of her dream plan was unattainable. That plan was to race Kona in October 2007, then Ironman World Championships 70.3 in Clearwater, Florida, four weeks later, followed by the Jamaica marathon in December before heading to England to spend Christmas with her family for the first time since she emigrated to Australia more than 30 years ago.

Weeks after her traumatic DNF and her decision to retire from Ironman, Kate spoke to Gillian, a close friend of 25 years. "Gillian knows I am challenged sometimes with my own propensity to put myself down and be negative. She encouraged me to do a blueprint of what I would need to do to fundamentally get my dream on the road," Kate says.

Kate learnt that the Ironman 70.3 Hawaii race in June offered one Kona spot in her age group. "I had to win."

Kate also needed three months off work and about $25,000. "When my boss said he'd give me the time and the bank said they'd give me the money, I decided to have another go at trying to qualify for Kona."

Triathlon became part of Kate's life only recently. At the age of 30, she'd started running after she gave up smoking. She ran two marathons, developed shin splints and was told she should never run again. So she took up cycling, loved it and stuck with it. "I competed in cycling for about 10 years. I know how to ride a bike and I know how to work with the bike," Kate says.

When Kate turned 50 she wanted to do a triathlon. She got some advice about running and learnt that nothing prevented her from doing so. "In fact, I have discovered I am a good runner."

She added swimming, a challenge, to her training. She entered her first triathlon in 2001, a sprint race at Kurnell, south of Sydney. In April 2003, she lined up for her first Ironman and finished in 13:01:47 on a cold, wet and stormy day in Forster. She immediately claimed her spot to race again the following year. But that wasn't meant to be. Three weeks later Kate is seriously injured during a women's cycling race. "I almost lost my right hand. I smashed my wrist really badly."

Her arms were in plaster for 14 weeks. She had three operations and couldn't train for about a year. "Because of that accident I don't have a very strong upper body. Certainly my arms are not very strong."

Cycle races, which often require riding closely together, lost their appeal for Kate. "Since then I have never raced another cycling race - it is a psychological thing about riding in a bunch."

Then her sister suddenly died at the age of 52 and six months later a close friend passed away at the same age. Kate decided she should use her passion for triathlon to stay fit and healthy and make the most from life. "I don't want to be 75 or 80 in my dotage wishing I'd done all these things. I've got my health now. It could all change next year. That's life," Kate says.

She did Ironman Australia in Port Macquarie in April 2005. The following year, she raced in the 55-59 age group and claimed third place. Kona seemed within reach. In early November 2006, she secured a spot for Clearwater at the Port Macquarie Half Ironman. But qualifying for Kona proved more elusive at Ironman WA a few weeks later.

"It was the first time I'd done a flat course and I discovered I don't like it. I basically switched off at some point in the ride and stopped eating. So by the time I got to the run when you have the voices in your head saying, `This is too painful, let's walk now or let's give up now', I actually listened to that voice. I couldn't even walk straight. I had chest pains and the doctor pulled me out. It was a combination of I was physically done, I didn't follow my plan - not eating - and also I let negativity take over," Kate says.

Reminded by her friend Gillian that she could still realise her 2007 dream plan, Kate switched coaches and joined the TriSpecific squad of Kristian Manietta in January. The next month Kate won her age group at the long course triathlon in Huskisson.

Kate renewed her commitment to triathlon and to reaching Kona with the help of her new coach. "Every coach is different. I knew Kristian would challenge me with my mental attitude which can be a bit negative. I'd listen to the voice in my head that said, `This is too hard, just stop.' He challenged me to see that I was a good athlete, that I had potential and that I could win. I had to do the footwork but I had to believe I could do it.

"That was sometimes the hardest thing, to believe I was actually capable of doing it. I didn't know how much he was going to push me physically but I realised I could go a lot further," says Kate.

Her win in Huskisson set the tone for following races. "As I won each race, my confidence got better and as that happened, Kristian would challenge me more physically. We did some incredible workouts on the weekend. I'd just almost fall over reading it [on the program], let alone doing it. But I would turn up and do it," Kate says.

One of Kate's training partners is Kristian's wife, professional triathlete Charlotte Paul who in November 2007 smashed the course record at Ironman WA by finishing in 9:00:55.

Charlotte says that one day she and Kate were the only two who came to a training session. It had been raining and was forecast to rain some more. "It was miserable. Kate had baked flapjacks to give to anyone who turned up. It was just her and I. It started to rain and I was over it, so I pulled the pin. She stayed and finished off that set," Charlotte says.

Kate was also working hard on her mindset. Her close-knit training squad was very supportive but had little patience for any negativity. "I was constantly on guard about changing that attitude."

Kate trained at least 20 hours a week, waking at 3.45am to stretch, then swim, ride and/or run before arriving at work at about 7.30am. Her boss, a cardiologist, is flexible about when Kate starts her eight-hour day. After work she'd often train again. Bedtime was 8pm. "Especially as I get older I have a 15-minute stretching routine in the morning that I do religiously. I'd rather get up earlier and do that, than stiffen up and not be able to train. I can be hard on myself in that way," Kate says.

Coach Kristian agrees. "She sometimes lacks a little belief but she is as hard as nails," Kristian says.

Kate swam three times a week, including squad workouts and one swim of 3 to 4 kilometres. She rode on two weekdays. She did 5-kilometre runs straight after those rides, which her coach didn't know. On Saturday the squad rode long, about 150 to 160 kilometres, including time trials of between 20 and 40 kilometres.

"Everybody was stronger and faster than me. Even just getting to Waterfall [about 45km from the start point in Centennial Park in Sydney] I had to push myself to stay with them. Eventually I'd get dropped but I was getting stronger just by trying to stay longer with a stronger group," Kate says.

Kate did her long run on Sundays. She also, reluctantly, did a weekly track run. "I really don't like running around in circles. But I persevered. I didn't miss more than two sessions. I improved with my pacing, and to race and be out of my comfort zone and to maintain that."

At Ironman 70.3 Hawaii in June, Kate won her age group and her prized Kona slot. She stayed for a Chris McCormack training camp. "I spent about four grand just doing that but I won - I got the spot. Once I'd done that, I just said to my boss, `Well what about it? Can I take all this time off to do these three events and then go home for Christmas?' And he was fantastic. My aim was to win but you never know."

Kate planned a three-month trip that included racing two world championships, and took out the remainder of her $25,000 bank loan. "I didn't want to end up regretting that I'd never tried and I thought, 'Well bugger it - I am just going to do it'."

Her big training sessions, her coach's focus on boosting her self-confidence and changing her mental attitude as well as her recent string of wins helped her cope with the inevitable tough moments. "I hear the voices but I counter it by saying, I am just going to go up this hill or just got to ride the next 5 kilometres,' and I focus on the race plan. I stay in the now and when that negativity comes, I remember the races where I have done really well," Kate says.

Even the best preparation and mental attitude are no guarantee. While Kate loved finally being able to race in Kona, infected blisters forced her to walk. She finished sixth in her age group in 13:33:53. Despite the painful setback, she says, "Kona was an amazing experience."

After Kona she went to San Francisco for the annual meeting of the Federation of Gay Games. She did some light training on her own. When she arrived in Florida she could refocus.

"I went to the race thinking I am just going to have fun and if I can get on the podium, I'd be really pleased," Kate says.

Missy LeStrange, World Triathlon Corp's 1999 age grouper of the year and holder of many course records, was one of the 14 women in her age group. Race morning was cold.

"Luckily the water was flat, flattish anyway. Two days before, it was really rough and I was right off course and really worried I wouldn't even make the cut-off. So when the swim was over I felt good," says Kate.

Kate thought she was about seventh out of the water in her age group. She doesn't wear a watch or heart rate monitor in races. "I much prefer to race not knowing what time it is so I can just concentrate on the race and not be distracted by this watch."

During the first part of the ride, she was passed by many younger age groupers. After the turnaround the wind picked up. Kate had passed about five women in her age group on the bike with about 5 kilometres to go.

"Then I saw Missy. I thought, oh my god what do I do now? So I just kept riding and prepared to get off the bike as you do in the last couple of kilometres. I thought, now the race is on."

Kate left T2 about 90 seconds before Missy. The run course was two laps. At the halfway point, "I could see Missy was chasing me and she was serious. I'd probably gained a minute but I was starting to slow down. I was determined not to stop."

Kate didn't know her age group position as no wristbands were given to competitors to mark completed laps.

"I really was hurting a lot. I thought I was at least in the top five and I was in front of Missy. I so much wanted to stop but I just kept thinking, I just got to get to the next aid station and don't stop in that aid station. Grab a drink and keep running. I'd break the race down or think of a positive experience that would alleviate the pain for five minutes. And keep doing it like that."

About 10 minutes after Kate finished, Missy congratulated her. "I had no idea why she was saying that," says Kate, unaware she'd become world champion. At the awards night Missy challenged her to come back in 2008 so they could race again.

"It was nice to win it against a legend like Missy LeStrange," Kate's coach, Kristian, says.

"Kate is a world champ because of her commitment and dedication to doing the work – training. Prior to Kona she came off her bike and ended up getting this huge hematoma [a collection of blood] on her thigh. She needed to get this drained a few times and it wouldn't have been the most comfortable thing to train with. But she turned up session after session. I believe she could win Kona but that is up to her to decide," Kristian says.

Kate ran the Jamaica marathon three weeks later in 4:08, winning her age group. Then she visited friends and family in Ireland and England. While her family is proud of her efforts, they can't relate. "They are so not into sports. They congratulate me but they think it is really weird and they don't understand why I do it. I just hope to inspire other people to do something active. As we get older our health is just so vitally important. When we train hard and look after our health, each day is a gift. Life is very precious and at our age you are always surrounded by people who are dying. So I just don't take my health for granted and I respect people who actually, no matter what they do in old age, have the vitality and energy that people who lead passive lives lack. That is worth a million dollars," says Kate.

Kate doubts she'll be able to return to Clearwater in 2008. "Of course it all comes down to money which I don't have. I claimed my spot. The way things are standing now, I won't be able to afford it but you just keep your options open. Maybe I'll sell my car," Kate says.

She's grateful for support already received, such as from bike shop Ashfield Cycles. "For two years they've been lending me race wheels every time I compete, helping me pack and set up my bike when I travelled, fixed my bike quickly when I needed it and given me spare parts and labour all at reduced costs. In return I have been making them cookies and cakes which they love."

While challenging at times, Kate's journey towards supreme fitness, self-confidence and making the most of the present has been very rewarding in many ways.

"The trophy [for winning the World Championship 70.3] is fantastic. It is the Mdot, very big in this beautiful aqua blue and the dot is red. It has your name and where you came in your age group. It is a stunning trophy and one I will treasure forever and who knows maybe I will get to defend it next year."

(First published in Australian Triathlete in 2008)

CHAPTER 9

Bernie Millett has been a runner for nearly six decades and is about to run his 45th marathon, a distance he has covered as fast as 2:32:47 in 1981. The 65-year-old holds several age-group records in Australian Capital Territory rankings on distances ranging from 800 metres to 42.195 kilometres.

Bernie is also one of eight Burley Griffins, or people who have completed at least 20 Canberra marathons. Bernie has run 23 and aims to make that 24 on April 15*. His marathon career spans three decades. The first time he took more than three hours to run one was only five years ago, finishing the 2002 CM in 3:01:32. A year he crosses the same finish line six seconds faster and runs a swift 3:00:06 in 2004 at the age of 62, the fastest person older than 52 on the day.

But he wasn't born a runner, he says. As a kid in the UK he participated in a cross country event he remembers very well. "I came last and I didn't like that," Bernie says. So he starts running. When he is 14 his family emigrates from the UK to Queanbeyan, Australia, where he does another cross country race. "I won that one," he says.

He joins a running group in Canberra, though he says a running group at that time was four people. In January 1958, Bernie joins the Australian Army as an apprentice. "That is when my running career really took off," he says. Bernie competes for the Army team in the annual cross country and track events.

"I could break two minutes for 800 metres on most days." His best mile time is 4:34, though he says "I was never really elite."

Bernie leaves the army in 1967 and re-establishes his contacts with runners in Canberra. "Jack Pennington was really responsible for kicking off the Canberra running scene," Bernie says. (Jack Pennington competed in the 1972 Munich Olympic Games, was ranked the world's No. 2 veteran athlete (age 50-55) until 1978 and was awarded the Australian Sports Medal in 2000.)

Bernie marries in 1968 and for a few years "did not really run that competitively". He does keep up his training. He joins the Department of Defence in 1971 and has several running colleagues. "There was quite a good group and we used to go out for lunch-time runs. Being in a running group you want to stay fit. After a while it becomes an addiction."

He starts to keep a record of his training in 1974, logging his daily runs, and still keeps track today. In January 1974, he runs 90 kilometres and increases that to 190 kilometres by January 1975. His training volume jumps again in 1976 when he decides to prepare for his first marathon, in Sydney. His marathon training program is to run, and run some more. "There wasn't much scientific thought that went into training. We did a longish run in those days but it wasn't long enough."

Race etiquette in the 1970s is strict, making for an interesting start. "We all lined up. The starter wouldn't fire the gun until everybody had tucked their singlets in their shorts," Bernie says.

Bernie finishes his first marathon in 2:51 and learns a few lessons. "I should always have a good pair of shoes. Mine looked nice but they were a bit too tight." He loses all his toenails after that race. That doesn't stop him from entering the first Canberra Marathon on a November afternoon in the same year. In October, he completes 576 kilometres of training and these pay off. "From memory I finished fairly strong."

Indeed, the then-35-year-old finishes in 2:49:36, seventh out of 17, and 13 minutes behind the 23-year-old winner John Harding.

Being a long-distance runner is unusual then. Bernie gets "some weird calls and looks" on his runs around Canberra. It is also hard to find information on how to train. He says training in the 1970s and 1980s is simply running as much as you can. "In the early years I really didn't know how to train. I don't think a lot of people did. Then there were people like [Steve] Prefontaine who were starting to put in huge mileages and everyone sort of started copying them, tried to get in the maximum mileage. Generally I'd just go out on the hard-day, easy-day principle, apart from trying to get in long runs every week."

He also looks at training methods by Austrian-born Franz Stampfl, who wrote the 1955 On Running book, had coached Roger Bannister and was recruited by Melbourne University, and Percy Cerutty, who trained Herb Elliott from 1956 to 1962. Bernie got first-hand tips. "Cerutty came to Canberra and gave us a lecture. I remember him doing all these push-ups, on his fingertips and toes."

So Bernie runs seven days a week which includes two runs some days to get his mileage up. He aims for 32 kilometres in his weekly long run and another 24 kilometres mid-week. The races he enters are his "only sort of speed work", he says. Such as for example a half marathon he does in 72:57 in 1979, his best time over the distance. He does train to run faster in the second half a run than the first. "I'd do an out and back course. I'd go out and then push it home as hard as I could."

While he also runs on trails in the forest, Bernie always does most of his marathon preparation on the road. "If you are going to run a marathon, you've got to train on a hard surface to get your body used to the pounding. So I think you have got to put in the long runs on the hard surface."

Occasionally he really goes off-road and runs the 90-odd kilometres between Perisher and Kiandra in Kosciuszko National Park with a group several times. It takes them between 9 1/2 and 11 hours. "We'd start at the Snowy River Hotel at 7am and run all day. We'd have bum bags and we'd be off in singlets and hoped that storms didn't come in."

In 1977 he again enters the Canberra Marathon, a Pacific Games trial marathon that year, and lowers his time to 2:47:20. "I wouldn't say I was happy," Bernie says, because he had run 2:44 in the Sydney marathon a few months earlier. For the year he runs 3500 kilometres.

In 1978, he signs up for a June marathon in Nowra. In the build-up to this race he runs 400 kilometres a month for five months and finishes in a new personal best of 2:41:34. He also runs the Canberra Marathon again in November and improves his time to 2:38:11, finishing 14th out of 189 runners. The first women participate in the race that year and Susan Hill comes home first in 2:59:38. Bernie ends 1978 having run 3663 kilometres.

In 1979 he runs three marathons (a feat he repeats in the following eight years with the exception of 1986 when he does two) and boosts his running volume to 3955 kilometres. He drops his Canberra Marathon time to 2:36:33. In 1980 his running reaches 4000 kilometres, completing the Adelaide marathon and Surfers Paradise within one month.

He remembers Surfers Paradise for three reasons: the event starts at 6am, the conditions are extremely humid and his family comes to watch him race. Bernie is the only runner in the family.

"You have to manage it," he says, referring to what they think of his running lifestyle. Bernie finishes in 2:39.

Distance running requires focus, Bernie says. While he enjoys other sports such as cycling and rogaining, during his marathon training he always concentrates on one thing only.

"You have to dedicate yourself to running. You don't get the time or the energy to do other sports," says Bernie.

One of the main changes he has seen in marathons is that the number of top runners has shrunk. "I have noticed with the Canberra marathon for instance that there were a lot more higher-end runners back 10, 15, 20 years ago then there are now. I mean you still have got really good runners up the front but there are not as many of them. I don't know whether that is caused by a lot of people maybe taking up triathlons and things like that rather than dedicating themselves just to running," Bernie says.

Dedicated runners or not, the number of participants has been going the right way. In 1997 the Canberra Marathon had 335 finishers, the lowest number since 1979. In 2006, 866 finished, the highest since the 1984 record of 1754.

Bernie's biggest year is 1981 when he completes 4692 kilometres, or an average 90 kilometres a week, and sets his best marathon time crossing the Canberra finish line in 2:32:47. "That was my easiest marathon. It didn't hurt too much."

Of course, as most runners would, Bernie wonders: "Could I have gone faster?"

As the kilometres add up in his training log - he writes daily notes on cards which he transfers to a book at the end of each month - for a while an obsession with numbers gets the better of him. When he finds himself at a weekly record of 98 miles (he'd log his training sometimes in miles, sometimes in kilometres), he can't help but do the extra 2 miles to complete the century. He has also run every single day in one year but has found a way to avoid that one. "Just to make sure I don't do that again, I take every January 1 off," he says.

The first time he doesn't improve his Canberra Marathon time is in 1982 when he runs 2:40:03. He blames it on "not getting to the finish line in time" and says he can't remember why "I went so slow".

His first DNF is in 1983 as the then-41-year-old is forced to pull out of the Canberra Marathon with an injury which he says was either calf or quad-related. He is back the next year when the Canberra Marathon is an Olympic trial and draws a record field, with 1754 finishers. Lisa Martin (now Ondieki) is the first female home in 2:35:05. Bernie runs in the same pack as Lisa.

"I was right there for a long time," says Bernie, who finishes in 2:38:10.

He always tries to find others running at the same pace. "You tend to get yourself in a pack moving at your speed and you stay there until you drop off or the pack drops off," Bernie says.

For him the most difficult part of the marathon is the first five kilometres as he tries to "get my pace in and get my breathing going. I usually drop off a bit between 15 to 20 kilometres before getting a second wind. I usually finish fairly strongly."

In his early marathons he would simply drink some water but later he starts mixing his own glycogenic drinks. He has one after 10km and "definitely one" after 35km, if he can stomach them. More recently, he has taken to energy gels. "I'll carry the one gel to have when I start dropping off. It would weigh me down to carry more."

Bernie's post-marathon recovery consists of taking the next day off, then "jog a bit and after three to four days you'd be OK, probably a bit flat." Another strategy is a two-week bike ride, usually after the Canberra Marathon. They bring tents and, yes, he does pack his running shoes too.

His 1985 Canberra Marathon goes by in 2:42:54, and he is 42nd out of 823 finishers. "Very humid, that's all my notes say about this race," Bernie says.

In 1986 he wants to get back into the 2:30s. "If I'd get the kilometres up, generally I'd run a good time." He says that meant then running at least 400 kilometres a month for a few months before the race. He finishes the Canberra Marathon in 2:42:20 that year, 28th out of a field of 823. From 1987, he no longer runs three marathons a year. "We started getting sensible."

But he always aims to do the Canberra Marathon. From 1987 when he is 45 until 2001 when he is 59, his Canberra Marathon times are between 2:48:46 and 2:59:58.

Bernie held the top spot in the 55-59 age group in the ACT marathon rankings from 1999 until 2007 with his 1999 finish Canberra Marathon time of 2:53:24, which was 10 minutes ahead of the second person. When he is 60, he finishes Canberra in 3:01:32, 64th out of 610 finishers. He grabs the ACT marathon top rank for the 60-65 age group with his 2004 Canberra finish time of 3:00:06, which is more than 13 minutes clear of No. 2. (Still current as of December 2009).

In 2006, and 30 years after his first Canberra Marathon, he runs his 23rd in Australia's capital, finishing in 3:21:26 at the age of 64. A calf injury four weeks before the race interrupts his training and he has to resort to riding his bike as preparation. His average Canberra Marathon finish time is 2:50:29, according to the Griffins list. "I'll always try to get under 3 hours," he says.

He moves up an age group in 2007. You might say he is gunning for the top ACT ranking spot in his new age group, which is 3:32:52, set by Ernie Warner in the 1998 Gold Coast marathon. However, training hasn't been going according to plan.

100

"I am feeling very sluggish this year," Bernie says. (As of December 2009, Bernie's 2007 Canberra Marathon finish time of 3:13:54 has him ranked the top runner in the 65-69 age group, 19 minutes ahead of No. 2).

Bernie is retired and while that may mean in theory that he has more time to run, he finds injuries restrict the amount of running he can do. His training volume started coming down in the 1990s. "I was getting older and the legs weren't taking the distance as much so I was easing back."

He has eased his training pace as well to about 12kph "if I am lucky" now, compared with about 16kph "in the early days".

Bernie still ran a half marathon in 1:35:08 in 2006. Barring injuries, he runs six days a week now, including one 30-kilometre one and the rest are between 7 and 10km. He still doesn't do a lot of speed work in training. "I reserve that for the race," he says.

He is trying to get a niggling Achilles under control and hasn't registered for the 2007 Canberra Marathon yet. "I usually register last minute because I never know when I will get injured again."

In the week before a marathon Bernie pays extra attention to his nutrition. "I eat fairly normally but maybe just a bit more carbohydrates." He stays away from "onions and things like that".

On race morning, Bernie gets up at about 5am. He'll have a Powerbar and a cup of tea. "Then I usually go to the race with a thermos of coffee. As I am sort of sitting around waiting I might have a coffee, black with no sugar. There is a theory that coffee is supposed to release the energy out of the fat in your body - I don't know how true that is."

The most important ingredient in running a good marathon is knowledge of which speed you will be able to maintain, Bernie says. "Of course you have to know what your capabilities are. You go out with a pace in mind - although I find myself that I can get through the first kilometres with the adrenalin pumping and you can use that to your advantage maybe for a little while. But you have got to settle down quickly at what should be your cruising speed because I believe it pays to run them steady. You can't, or at least I couldn't, surge. I get up to my main speed and stay there."

*Bernie ran the Canberra Marathon in 2007 in 3:13, 2008 in 3:19 and 2009 in 3:16.

(First published in Run For Your Life in 2007)

CHAPTER 10

Karen Scott took up running at the age of 34 and realised she wasn't the un-athletic person she had always considered herself to be. Six years later Karen finished her first marathon at the Gold Coast in a better-than-expected 3 hours and 26 minutes. "The feeling of running down that finishers' chute brings tears to my eyes and makes my heart beat faster even now, two years later. It was euphoric. Nothing in my life has ever been close to that awesome feeling of achievement," Karen says.

That was July 2006 and Karen was on top of the world. But in February 2007, six months after achieving that milestone, a chronic hamstring injury stopped Karen from running and doing any exercise altogether. Only a year later, in 2008, was Karen slowly recovering from her injury with the help of experimental blood injection treatments. She has accepted and learnt to deal with the physical pain of her injury. She's had a much tougher time with losing the ability to run and coping with the uncertainty of if, when and how she can return to the sport that has become a huge part of her life.

"It has been the toughest 12 months, emotionally, that I have ever endured. I tried immersing myself more in work, trying other non-physically active hobbies, but nothing even comes close to what running gives me. Running is my identity - I am a runner. Without it I feel less than human. My confidence and self-esteem have taken a battering since I have been injured. I have suffered periods of depression, stress and emotional highs and lows. I have sought the help of a sports psychologist during this time, and he has helped a great deal, but I know I won't feel real again until I am running again," says Karen.

Despite initially being told her injury meant her running days were over, Karen is determined to return to the unlikely passion she only discovered in her 30s. "I used to be the queen of sleep-ins, although I was always conscious of my appearance. In high school I took up jogging on a bush track next to my family home but I'm sure this only lasted a number of weeks. I avoided sports carnivals at school and hated team sports, as I felt I didn't fit in and lacked the required skills to participate. I was the kid to always get picked last for a team; it was total humiliation which did nothing to boost my poor self-esteem at the time. I occasionally went through fads of taking up aerobics here and there, but that was about it. I weighed about 60 kilograms [she is 161 centimetres] within three years of getting married and thought I was just destined to be like that forever, because I didn't consider myself to be the sporty type."

Karen changed her mind – and body - when she and husband Neil bought a five-acre block of bush land in Martinsville, NSW, on the side of a steep ridge and started building their own home in 1997. At the same time she also began a low-fat diet. "To build our dream home - a pole home - we first had to clear the building site which meant some really hard yakka over many, many months. My body started to transform quite dramatically," Karen says.

In the three years it took the couple to build the house, Karen lost 7kg and gained plenty of energy. "I'd never before been that slim and fit – I looked trim, taut and terrific and felt great. Every day was spent working on our hillside carrying heavy loads up and down, climbing, lifting, pushing a heavy wheel barrow and of course building the house."

When they finished construction in 2001, Karen took up walking and aerobics to preserve her newfound fitness. She also bought a slew of exercise equipment: a treadmill, exercise bike, elliptical trainer, rowing machine, aerobic step, gym ball, mini trampoline, weights, boxing bags, skipping rope and at least 20 exercise tapes.

In September 2001 she did a 40-kilometre charity walk, split into two 20km stretches over two days, along the shores of Lake Macquarie. "I felt alive, fit, healthy and keen to continue with my new way of life."

Karen decided to enter her first fun run the next month, the 5km Race for Research on the Newcastle foreshore. "My training consisted of seeing how far I could run, without stopping, the afternoon before the race. I did about 3km, with a very red face and a lot of puffing. So the following day I bravely fronted for the event all on my own and proudly completed it in 30:01. I felt so independent and proud of myself and with that I was hooked on running."

In 2001 Karen placed 51st out of 387 participants in the open female category. She has run that race every year since (except 2007 because of her injury). In 2006 she did a PB of 21:30 and placed 10th out of 620 women. "After doubting my athletic ability my whole life, I finally discovered that not only could I run, but for someone taking it up so late in life, I was quite good at it and competitive in my age group. It has developed into a passion that dominates my life. Nothing else can come close to matching the feeling I get when I run and compete."

Karen trained hard and enjoyed seeing her run times get faster. Besides running five times a week, she rode her mountain bike, did aerobics, weight training and used her other home gym equipment. She got her first age-group placing in 2003, finishing third in the hilly 5km Lindfield Fun Run in 23:51. She also ran her first half marathon that year. "I was so competitive, I couldn't wait to enter as many races as I could find that were within travel distance from home."

In 2004, she earned her first age-group win in the Wallaroo Fun Run near Raymond Terrace. "I was thrilled to finally achieve a gold medal that wasn't just for participation."

Besides numerous running races, Karen also entered cycling events with husband Neil. In 2005, Karen set her half marathon PB of 96:30 in Lake Macquarie.

And then came 2006. "Of course 2006 is the highlight of my running career so far being the Year of the Marathon. Sadly that is also what led to my long-term injury."

Three earlier attempts to get to the start line of a marathon had failed, so finally being able to start and finish one meant a lot. Not to mention her fantastic time. "Nothing on earth could possibly feel better than achieving what only a year or two earlier seemed impossible. The intensity and sacrifices involved in training for a marathon are all worthwhile when you realise, in the last 3km, that you are about to complete the biggest challenge of your life so far. The high began when in the last 10km I ran past the pace group that I had thought I'd never be able to keep up with, and then finished four minutes ahead of them," says Karen.

Karen was back training within two days after the Gold Coast marathon, doing brisk walks. She decided to run the Melbourne marathon, held three months later. "I began running again on the fifth day after the Gold Coast but was still too sore in the quads during the 6km jog. So I went back to walking for another couple of days before beginning a full week of running and cross-training again. Within seven days I was doing speed-

and hill work, runs of between 8km and 14km, rode the exercise bike, lifted weights and did a 34km mountain-bike ride."

Eight weeks after her first marathon she was running more than 70km per week. Her longest runs were 36km which she did both in the ninth and tenth weeks. Then her body softly, but surely, started giving signs of protest. Karen sought treatment from her physiotherapist Brendan Clark, and acupuncture as well as weekly massage. "It was thought my problem was piriformis syndrome [a condition where the piriformis muscle irritates the sciatic nerve, causing pain in the buttocks and referring pain along the sciatic nerve] as my glute muscles were so tight and sore all the time."

She ran the Melbourne marathon in October 2006, finishing in 3 hours and 29 minutes. Again, she resumed training quickly. "I was regularly feeling pain in my left hamstring and both glutes but I still had only four days of complete rest. Within a week I was back to running, walking and cycling daily."

Early December, she finished the Tuggerah Lakes Festival half marathon in 1 hour and 40 minutes. The effort forced her to take a break from running. Instead, she did 10km walks and mountain-bike rides of up to two hours.

"There was no way I was giving in and losing my fitness due to a pain in the butt. After 11 days of cross-training I tried a couple of 16km runs, but I was in pain a lot of the time. Despite this, on Boxing Day 2006 I began an advanced marathon training program while my injury steadily became worse. I was advised by Brendan to cut back on my running by initially eliminating my long runs, but I stubbornly kept running distances up to 21km. He then told me to cut out all speed work and hill work, as my injury wasn't responding to treatment and continued to get worse.

"I just wasn't listening. Despite taking his advice by this time, I was still doing far too much and not listening to the signs my body was giving me. I eventually had to concede defeat and give up running altogether on February 19, 2007, when I got only 1km into a morning training run and broke down in pain. Even then, instead of walking home I jogged - talk about stubborn. By now I had a sports physician, physiotherapist, acupuncturist and massage therapist all trying to work out why my piriformis was giving me so much trouble and why it wasn't responding to any form of treatment."

In May 2007, she went to Sydney where an MRI showed a small tear in her left hamstring, bone marrow oedema at the junction of both hamstrings and bilateral hamstring tendinitis.

Her physio referred her to Brent Kirkbride, a sports physiotherapist at the Sydney Sports Medicine Centre. "Brent told me that he had treated several long distance runners around my age with this type of injury but mine was the worst case he had seen. He gave me little hope of ever running more than 10km again, but even that would take many, many months to achieve. I was devastated, heart broken, angry and lost. I couldn't believe that I, an ordinary runner without any special ability, could possibly end up with such a serious injury."

Karen was given a series of glute and hamstring strengthening exercises and nerve stretches. It was almost all she could do, as by then her hamstrings had become too painful to do any form of exercise. Initially she had continued her cross-training. "In February, when I was forced to stop running, I still believed it would just be a matter of weeks before I could run again. I started circuit training, skipping, high energy aerobics, and aqua aerobics and rode many kilometres on my mountain bike to try to compensate for the loss of running time and to desperately avoid gaining weight. I still ignored any signs that my legs were getting sorer, believing that any day they would start to show improvement: after all, I was no longer running and that is what caused the problem in the first place."

She decided to take took swimming lessons too. At first she could barely do one 25-metre lap, but within six weeks she could do 26 laps. "I was so proud of myself that I deemed 2007 to be the Year of the Swim. I felt that my injury must have been fate, just so I could finally learn to swim. However, all this was done without kicking, instead using a pull buoy and flippers for flotation."

However, it aggravated her injury and Karen had to stop swimming seven weeks after she started. "My hamstrings, particularly the left one which had the tear, were just so sore that I couldn't bend over, sit for more than 10 minutes or walk up stairs without pain. I couldn't even go outside for a short walk."

In August 2007, Brent told Karen about experimental autologous blood injections which had mostly been used in Melbourne to treat AFL players with similar injuries. Your blood has growth factors that can help healing in injuries of muscles, tendons and ligaments. These growth factors may lessen pain and disability and speed the recovery from injury.

Karen had the procedure done on her left leg. "Blood was taken from my arm and, guided by ultrasound, was immediately injected into the left hamstring after a local anaesthetic. After three weeks of total rest and five more of light exercise, my left leg was starting to feel less sore and I was gradually able to begin riding and doing aerobics again."

By January 2008 she could do three-hour mountain bike rides, lower body weights and even a few jogs of about 3km. Then she suffered another setback. "My right hamstring had started to become worse. So in mid-February, one year after first breaking down, I had blood injections into both hamstrings."

About a month after the procedure, Karen was able to ride the exercise bike, do upper body weights, and her leg and glute exercises. "My right leg is still quite painful and aches whenever I drive or sit for long periods. It will still be months before I can again try some short jogs but my physiotherapists are hopeful that I will be able to run short distances again one day. It sadly seems my passion for long distance running may never again be realised. I have been told to aim for triathlon instead, as it isn't as hard on the body. At the moment I'd just be happy to be able to walk out the door and do a slow 5km jog."

Dealing with her injury has been difficult. "During the last 12 months I have felt very lost, sorry for myself, miserable and low. I still haven't found anything that comes even close to filling the space that not being able to run has left in my daily life. It was a major part of a very active lifestyle and I miss it terribly. I ache when I see other people out running on my way to work. When travelling my favourite running routes I often wonder if I'll ever get to run them again."

She sought help from sports psychologist Paul Penna. "He has really helped me in dealing with my injury and my future – possibly in triathlon. I can't thank him enough: I am in a completely different and much happier headspace now compared to six months ago. He has helped me come to terms with the changes in my body since giving up running, which are really hard to accept. The emotional issue of injury is like a grieving process that takes time to work through.

"All my goals were running related and based on marathons and even ultras in the future. I now know that won't be possible. I feel that if I had listened to advice in the early stages of the running injury, it wouldn't have become as chronic as it did. If only I had taken weeks instead of days to rest properly after my first marathon. Hindsight is a wonderful thing. I've certainly learnt my lesson the hard way. If only I'd listened to my body when it started to feel tired and sore I'd probably still be running," says Karen.

While Karen will have to adjust her long-term running goals from marathons and beyond, to shorter runs and triathlons, she remains determined to run again. "Running has made me more confident, self-assured, independent, more driven and passionate. It has certainly changed my life dramatically, to say the least."

(First published in Run For Your Life in 2008)

CHAPTER 11

Alan Farrell is one of the 43 men who have run the hilly City to Surf race from Sydney's central business district to Bondi Beach each of the 36 years since 1971. Alan has run them fast. While the race is now 14 kilometres, it was a kilometre longer during the first few years of the event. "For my first 30, I always went under the hour," the 62-year-old says.

Alan says he didn't consider himself a real runner until after his third City to Surf. Yet, he did have high hopes for the first one. He ran as part of his training while serving as an Australian Army commando and he was also a member of the Norths Joggers club in Balmoral. He was told to keep a close eye on Olympian runner Kenny Moore from the United States (who ended up crossing the finish first).

"I had visions of winning the darn thing," Alan says.

"I was still with [Kenny] at 600 meters. By the time I got to the other side of the [Kings] Cross I was walking. I wasn't the only one. There were people hanging over fences. The ambulance guys had to do some work because people weren't fit. At Rose Bay I was saying 'never again'."

Alan finished and as he drove over the course that same afternoon, he changed his mind and decided he'd return the next year. "It is the greatest race in the world. It is certainly the best in Australia. It is a hard race. You've got the hills. There is no place you can settle down really."

Alan placed about 50th overall in the first few City to Surf races, then crossed the line in about 75th spot for several years before placing about 125th for four years, he says.

His best City to Surf performance was when he ran the then-15km course in 53:10, he says. At the time, the course started at Town Hall and there was no tunnel at Kings Cross. His best time for the 14km course is 50:07. He says he should have broken 50 minutes but it just didn't happen. "I was always around that 50 minutes. I should have gone under it. Friends of mine would go under it and I'd always beat them in runs but couldn't handle the City to Surf," he says.

Alan was one of the inaugural members of Sydney's Norths Joggers club, dubbed the Bears, which started in May 1967. "We'd run but not that sort of distance [15km]," he says.

His work kept him fit as well. "There was a lot of running in the commandos. We used to run along the promenade at Balmoral and there were complaints that running in our army boots was going to break up the path."

The Bears still can lay claim to having four City to Surf legends. Besides Alan, they are Laurie Coleman, Phil Worrall and John Tisdale. Alan gradually built up his running frequency, he says, but he had only one speed. "For the first 10 years of my running, it was all hard. People didn't run with me. It was at least

10 years before I realised that you don't have to run flat out every time," he says.

What Alan doesn't say is that he was in the Top 3 of the Norths Joggers men's open series almost every year. The club's website shows results from 1978 until 2005 and it is easier to count the years that Alan's name is missing from the Top 3 (1996 and 1997). His name last appears in the Top 3 in 1998 after which he moved to Runaway Bay in Queensland.

And even though he claims that his competitive spirit has lessened, it doesn't sound like it. In the 2005 City to Surf he finished in about 62 minutes, only 30 seconds behind the fastest legend Keith Mayhew.

Before the 2006 City to Surf, "Keith said to me 'I bet you are going to beat me this year' but the wheels fell off unfortunately. I had a bad run," Alan says, who finished in 68:00.

Keith ran 67:06. "We both crashed," Alan says.

Alan blames the move from Sydney to Queensland and the lack of hills to train on. His wife Carole has a better explanation. With as many women as men among the more than 63,000 entrants in 2006, Alan was simply distracted. In the first City to Surf there were only about 40 women among the 2000 entrants.

"My wife said I wasn't running well because I was stuck among all these pretty girls," Alan says.

In the first eight years of the City to Surf he always beat the first woman to the finish line. So he was taken aback when a female runner passed him going up Heartbreak Hill in the 1979 City to Surf. To make matters worse, he didn't recognise her. "I knew the top girls. I am looking at her and I said `What's your name?' She said `Lawrie' with an American accent. I am thinking who the bloody hell is Lawrie and I lost a bit of concentration as she disappeared from me. I found out her name was Lawrie Binder and she was an American Olympian," says Alan.

Lawrie was the first female home in 49:40 and the first woman to break 50 minutes on the course.

As for his wife, Alan considers her to be a City to Surf legend in her own right. "Carole has been to every City to Surf and she has had the hard part because she has had to drop us in the city, drive the car out and park it and it got further and further away" as the number of participants in the race grew, says Alan.

After bringing Alan to the race start, Carole and the kids would drive to the finish in Bondi. "Our ritual was that we would find somewhere to park, drag everything down to the beach, go to the fish 'n' chips shop and buy $2 worth of chips and milkshakes. Then we'd sit in the gutter by the finish and the kids would actually count the runners in" until Alan finished, Carole says.

"Even now the kids say `Mum don't forget to get your chips'," says Carole.

Running has definitely played a large part in the family's life. "That City to Surf definitely changed my lifestyle. I didn't expect when I ran that first one that I'd still be running 36 years later. It got me a job working in a gym for 23 years, all our social life. I love running and I have become addicted to it," Alan says.

When Alan switched his commando role for a job at Telstra, he'd run every lunch hour. "People would say to me 'what do you enjoy about work?' and I'd say the lunch hour. It was getting embarrassing. I'd get in the lift and people would say, G'day Alan where you have been? You been for a run or are you going for a run?"

Carole decided the whole family would support Alan wherever he went to run. "I figure that part of making a marriage work is sharing each other's interests. If I stayed at home, we'd probably drift apart," Carole says.

During the 1980s the family spent almost every weekend travelling to a running event. "I used to say to Carole 'Would you like to go away for a weekend?' And she'd say 'yeah, yeah, where is the run at?' 'Well, there is a run at Mudgee or there is a run at Lithgow'," Alan says. Fun runs became a large part of the family's social life. "We went away a lot and we made a lot of friends out of it. It just became a sociable day out with picnics so the kids had pretty healthy outings and weekends," Carole says.

Those runs included 13 marathons. Alan ran his first in 3:00:15 and finished the others in less than 3 hours. His fastest time is 2:50.

Alan also gradually changed his mental approach to the sport. "When I first started running, I used to just switch off. Then I realised that you really have to concentrate while you are running. You can drop places or anything can happen while you are thinking about something else."

His training schedule currently includes four runs and three deep-water running sessions a week. Carole is a keen walker - and organiser. After the Gold Coast Runners Club, which Alan joined after their move to Queensland, moved to Burleigh Waters, the couple set up a new one. "We thought there was a need for a club at the northern end of Broadwater," Alan says.

Carole is now president and secretary of the two-year old Southport Runners and Walkers Club while Alan is the club's captain. There are 150 members and a third of them turned out for the club's most recent run, Alan says.

The club had at least 20 members at this year's City to Surf. "Some people used to say to me, `It is all right for you – you get a preferred start'. I used to say, I get the preferred start* not because my name is Alan Farrell - I have to bloody earn it. But now I do get the preferred start because my name is Alan Farrell."

* Sydney's City to Surf is the world's largest timed fun run and drew more than 76,000 entrants in 2009. Runners with a preferred start are allowed to start behind the elite, so-called seeded, competitors. Alan ran again in 2007 in 67:39, 2008 in 67:15 and 2009 in 68:31.

(First published in Run For Your Life in 2006)

CHAPTER 12

Stephen Callahan sure wasn't born a runner. "I had never been interested in running - I avoided it studiously. Through my school years I often got my mum to write me a note getting me out of running because of mystery ailments if you know what I mean."

How times change. Many years and about 23 marathons later, the 52-year-old Stephen has three grown sons and says, "I keep saying to the boys that they won't become real men until they do a marathon. That gnaws away at them a bit."

Stephen himself changed his mind in his late 20s after he was forced to spend about 22 months during a three-year period off work because of two severe leg injuries. First, Stephen broke his leg in an unusual way. Having had a few drinks, he says he needed quite a bit of assistance to get out of a car. Unfortunately one of his legs got stuck in the process and he ended up with a broken fibula. It took him 14 months to recover.

"When I got out of plaster I thought I better get a bit fit so I started to do a bit of running."

Twelve months later Stephen crashed his motorbike and required an external fixation device on one of his legs. Screws are placed in the bone above and below a fracture, and a device is attached to the screws from outside the skin, where it may be adjusted to align the bone. It took him a couple of years to recover from that injury which cemented his earlier decision to take up running.

"Just the look of my whole leg was a bit of a shock. From 1986 I started to do a bit of jogging around. At about the same time I got married and had a few kids and sold the motorcycle - I had bought another motorcycle while I was in the hospital. It was a bargain. And then I got rid of it."

Stephen's renewed resolve to become a runner was hampered by stress fractures around the areas of his leg injuries. "I jogged for a while, ran around, and started running every third day, every second day and then tried every day. I'd get a bit sore so I'd back off a little bit. I had a few stress fractures because of where the original smashed tibula and fibula were. They weren't healing properly. It got a bit complicated unfortunately so I had to back off and I had to have bone graft and stuff like that."

By 1988 he felt fit enough to enter his first race and didn't mess around. Like the rest of Australia, Stephen was inspired by Robert de Castella's phenomenal performances. So Stephen decided his first race would be a marathon.

"I mean it is a good effort to run a 10km or a half but a marathon is the ultimate. For the first one, I was out in the bush on my own running about 30km three times a week. The training was ridiculous. But it gets into your head when you are out in the bush thinking about finishing a marathon and having your family there, that's I think where it all comes from. There is a real rush.

"Ten metres before the finish you feel exhausted and 10 metres after you feel fantastic," Stephen says.

He chose the Bicentennial Melbourne marathon, and finished in 3:10:12. Stephen won't be drawn on how that compared with his expectations. "I was just happy to finish because I saw death."

He forgot about that quickly enough and ran his second marathon in 1989. It was a steep learning curve. "After a solid year of training and running with the group I improved by about eight seconds the next year," Stephen says.

While he trained with and was guided by Gerry Surridge, who has represented Australia in marathons overseas, Stephen didn't always use common sense. "The week before a marathon I was out doing 500-metre sprints. I hadn't done that before but someone said, 'Have you been doing any sprints?' I hadn't so I went out and did some loops around the lake. That probably wasn't a great idea. You can see how non-scientific my approach was," Stephen says.

He kept at it, running about two marathons a year.

By 1997 Stephen had his training and racing skills down pat. The then-42-year-old broke 2:40 at both the Melbourne and the Gold Coast marathons including a PB of 2:37. He also ran his best half marathon and 10km times. His 10km PB is 32:24.

His half marathon PB is "about" 71 minutes: "It was supposedly a professionally measured course but they apologised and said it was about 200 metres short," says Stephen.

While he knows the most important statistics of his running career, he doesn't keep training logs. "I sort of started by writing it on the calendar just above the phone but after a while … I am not a very good record-keeper," Stephen says.

His fastest year came after a decade of hard training. Initially he'd set his sights on finishing a marathon in less than three hours, an achievement that is still one of his best marathon memories.

"I guess breaking three hours is always a personal triumph. I got around a 3:09, a 3:05, a 3:03, so I worked my way down. I think I did a 2:57 or something and I thought, 'That was enough. I am happy with that'. Of course a couple of months later I wanted to break 2:50 so I worked my down through the 50s. I did that at the Gold Coast and I was going to be happy with that. But I was still running with all these guys who were very competitive so I thought maybe I can go a bit quicker. They say 10 years of solid training will produce your best marathon for a person who is not specifically a super athlete. So I aimed at that and kept whittling away. I got down to 2:40. And then I went up to the Gold Coast and broke it up there."

Stephen says his PB came unexpected. "It was a 2000-km drive and I was staying with my brother-in-law who is a pastry cook so we ate well. Sometimes you can be in perfect nick and have a dud. And other times not feel good and have a great day."

He credits his wife Susan for helping him achieve those goals. "She's been a great support. With having three young kids and me heading off to go for a run with the guys on Sunday mornings for 2 1/2 to 3 hours, she was very tolerant. She knew I needed a bit of an outlet. It's very addictive and it's a feel-good thing to go out for a three-hour run through the bush, sniff the air and have a bit of a chat with your friends. When you come home you might be exhausted and a bit crippled, but it certainly puts you in a better frame of mind."

Susan is a keen walker. While she rarely runs, she won a medal when she placed first veteran in a 5km run at the Gold King festival. As for their three sons who are 18, 20 and 22, "they certainly haven't followed my lead at all. When they were young they were probably reasonably impressed when they were dragged around to watch me finish marathons. Now they just shake their heads and walk away and have a bit of a laugh at the silly old bugger I think. That's all right. They'll do it one day."

He's been encouraging others including colleagues Anne and Tracey who have taking up running. Stephen finds he often has to tell novice runners to take it easy.

"Some tend to get a bit carried away with it and you don't want them to get injured because then they won't do it at all."

By 1998 Stephen started venturing into multi-sport and ultra events with his "adventure racer coach and co-competitor" Eric Van Doorn. They did a two-day race from Mt Buller to Melbourne in a team of three. Each team cycled, ran and paddled together on both days. "That was a very tough event. We used to go very well in that."

He also tried his hand at Ironman triathlon, which involves swimming 3.8km, cycling 180.1km and running a marathon. Stephen did his one and only Ironman at Forster-Tuncurry in 2000. "I got that out of the way and wouldn't go back to that one. I overtrained for it as usual and I had a bad run which should have been my best leg."

Still he made the most of the marathon by eating and drinking everything that was on offer at the Ironman aid stations. "I thought I can't do anything so I'll get my money's worth. I ate pretty well that day. I think I put on weight."

Stephen preferred the Upper Murray Challenge - a mix of mountain biking, paddling and running - even though he had a few mishaps. "I busted my nose in one, and got myself knocked out." The latter resulted in a trip to the hospital.

He favours the simplicity and the sensation of running over multi-sport events. "There's the convenience of going for a run compared with mucking around when you are going for a paddle or riding a bike. You don't get the buzz from doing those sorts of things as you do from going for a run through the forest."

So Stephen is still running, with many of the same people he began more than 20 years ago, like his brother Julian, Gerry Surridge, Graeme Allen, Robert Gray, Mike Gustus and Rob Soar.

Julian started running a year after Stephen. "My brother and I have had a friendly rivalry over the years. I am well on top I might add. He is a lot more talented but lacks ticker. We're past our prime as far as marathons go for speed so are getting into the ultra stuff now."

Another brother Phillip, nicknamed Ned, recently broke a running drought of more than 30 years following his first and only marathon at the age of 22. Last year, the 55-year-old ran the 10km Rip to River. "It's never too late," Stephen says.

Stephen is training for his sixth Trailwalker, held annually, in which a team of four covers 100km on foot to raise money for Oxfam. Stephen's team, Best Boys, is usually among the top finishers and is preparing for the April 2008 Oxfam Trailwalker Melbourne. It also includes Julian, Graeme and Robert, with Mike as reserve. Gerry is sidelined by injury. "We have got a great crew - you're only as good as the crew that is around you. We've known each other for about 20 years so any differences have been ironed out a long time a go. It's about encouraging each other."

The weekly training distance for Trailwalker will be as high as 150km by March and involves several 50km races as preparation. In the Mansfield to Mt Buller 50km race on January 27, Julian was second overall in 4:38:33 and Stephen was third in 4:42:13. Even Stephen concedes that Julian is running well at the moment. This race starts at an altitude of 1200 feet and climbs to 2000 feet by 32.6km. Then the fun begins with a 4000-foot climb for the next 15km, before dropping 600 feet for the final 2km.

Stephen doesn't see himself entering any runs that are longer than 100km. "If it wasn't for Trailwalker, a team event, I wouldn't do it because it takes too much of an edge off your speed and times."

And there's another reason. "They're a pretty weird bunch, the people who do ultras. They are good people but certainly a little bit left of centre," Stephen says.

Instead, Stephen may do something a bit more normal, like running another Gold Coast marathon in July. "See how I pull up from Trailwalker."

(First published in Run For Your Life in 2007)

CHAPTER 13

Running a marathon is a big undertaking, whether it is your first or fifth. The key to success is preparation and most runners will benefit from enlisting an experienced running coach who can set up a customized training program. While training plans and philosophies vary from coach to coach, they agree on one thing: a runner's motivation and attitude are crucial.

"When I am talking to a guy about a marathon, certainly out of our group, you assess for that little twinkle in the eye," says Dave Scott-Thomas, head coach of athletics at the University of Guelph. "You have to really want to do it."

And that goes for anyone - from Dave's elite athletes such as Calvin Staples, who ran 2:24:20 in the 2007 Ottawa marathon or Taylor Murphy, who ran 2:24:59 in the 2008 Ottawa marathon, to a recreational runner who just wants to finish that 42.195 kilometres.

Marathon Dynamics coach Kevin Smith says, "It's internal resolve. There are going to be 100 moments of self-doubt, so there have to be 101 moments of reaffirmation, of positive optimistic can-do attitude."

A typical marathon training program is 16 to 20 weeks, though of course much depends on running experience and current training volume. Kevin generally advises athletes work their way up progressively through the different race distances, starting with a 5km race. A novice runner may take two years before they run a marathon, he says, adding that there are exceptions. While the planning horizon for Dave's elite athletes consists of years rather than months – they are already thinking about the 2012 London Olympic marathon – the final build-up for a marathon is also about 16 to 20 weeks, Dave says.

Kevin provides customised training programs for runners of any ability. To Kevin, an intermediate marathoner has already completed between two and five marathons. Regardless of race experience and current training volume, Kevin's athletes will do no more than four runs a week to maximise rest and recovery. The length and intensity of those runs will vary per runner. This intermediate plan peaks at 66km a week. The average weekly volume on Kevin's plans is about 40km to 45km, he says.

"One of the more defining characteristics of our approach is minimalist frequency. It's more about efficient mileage for training volume, than seeing how much your body can take. The magic is in the pacing," he says.

Kevin's programs consist of three key runs. If a fourth is included, it's an active recovery run, rather than an ability-enhancing one. "Every run is very different – they each have their own distinct purpose. The big three are your three elements: endurance, strength and speed. One run is your long slow distance (LSD) and the purpose is to ensure that you can cover the distance of your chosen event – it is the time-on-your-feet run.

"The other key element is your intensity workout. The purpose is to change the potential finishing time or to change the potential speed that you can run at," Kevin says.

The third weekly key run is what Kevin has termed the Ordinary Mortal Pace (OMP) run. "That reinforces your ability to carry the speed you have over the distance you are trying to run. It's a little faster than your current forecast or prescribed marathon race pace, and it's a little slower than your current half marathon pace," he says.

Dave Scott-Thomas's group of elite athletes include Canada's best 5000m and 10,000m runners. "A number of those athletes are moving into the marathon," he says.

For non-elite runners, he considers a 3:00 marathoner advanced for men and about 3:15 for women. While his athletes run up to 190km a week in preparation for a marathon, Dave also focuses on other aspects like nutrition, recovery and mental training. He recommends every marathoner practice race nutrition and hydration in training. (And Kevin agrees with that, providing specific recommendations for each of his athletes.)

Dave says, "The marathon is long enough that I don't think anybody can undertake it lightly. In fact if you're looking at people who are running 4 or 5 hours the energy system that they use is quite different - and in a way more complex - than a real advanced marathon runner. Your intake of calories and fuel during the competition is supercritical. You really need to practice that and be smart about it, otherwise you are going to hit the infamous bonk. And that's painful and no fun."

Dave's marathon training programs have three-week cycles, with two higher volume weeks followed by a week with a 15 to 20 per cent drop in volume. That may include a day without running. "The differences are critical. So for example a progression might be doing 90 miles one week, 110 the next, 120 miles the next, and the following week bumping back down to 95, and then going back up to 120 for a couple of weeks," he says.

Dave says the taper, or reduction in training volume before a goal race, on the programs he provides his athletes is short.

"We tend to hold our volume fairly close to the actual race time, then drop down fairly quickly. So even four weeks out from Chicago, Calvin [Staples] ran 100 miles that week. But then he brought it down fairly quickly in succession down to 75 miles, and 65 and then 40 miles preceding," Dave says.

Tempo workouts are a key component. "In general I would say a lot of training plans would have people going too short and too fast in the marathon. So we're often doing things like 70 minutes worth of tempo work," Dave says.

A Sunday 20-mile run may include a 40-minute tempo and a 30-minute tempo session, he says. "We're making sure that they are staying sub-threshold. So that's a relatively gentle workout.

"It's certainly marathon race pace and maybe a little bit faster than that," says Dave.

Another important component is preparing the mind for the marathon. In the last couple of years, mental training has become more practical, Dave says. "We model a lot in practice."

For example, his athletes will run four times 5km on the road with 3 minutes in between and project each repeat for different stages of a marathon. "So the first 5km here's how we want you to think: You're going to be in with a crowd of guys, and here's how you are going to feel - let's do some visualisation. As they're training, they are trying to create that association with how we imagine the race is going to unfold. So in a practical sense we are trying to do that all the time. Today's workout is designed to get you to that long lonely feeling that you have at the end of the race, physiologically but also psychologically."

First-time marathoners may consider a program such as offered on the Royal Victoria Marathon website. The 23-week plan, maintained and developed by two-time Olympic marathoner Bruce Deacon, prepares novice marathoners to complete the distance using a 9-minute run, 1-minute walk approach. To follow this program you should be comfortable completing 8 to 10 miles using the run-walk approach. Training involves run-walk sessions on 4 days a week.

You may replace one of these training days - except the long run - with alternative aerobic exercise like cycling, swimming or water running. All sessions should be done following the 9-minute/1-minute approach, unless otherwise specified.

(First published in Canadian Running magazine in 2008)

About the author

Margreet Dietz was born in 1970 in The Netherlands. After obtaining a Bachelor of Commerce, she began a career in marketing only to realise that what she really wanted to do was to write. She quit her job in 1995 and went back to university, moving to Brussels, Belgium, where she obtained a post-graduate degree in International and European Law at the University of Brussels. In 1996 she started working as a reporter at Bloomberg News in its Brussels office, followed by stints in Toronto, Canada, and subsequently Sydney, Australia. She left Bloomberg News in March 2004 to travel and compete in endurance sports events around the world including three Ironman triathlons. In 2006 she was hired as a copy-editor at The Australian Financial Review in Sydney, and began writing for endurance sports magazines. She and long-time partner Tim moved to the West Coast of Canada at the end of 2007, where she started researching and writing her first book, *Running Shoes Are a Girl's Best Friend*, published in November 2009. Margreet now lives with Tim and their dog Luka in Squamish, BC, where the five-time Ironman finisher is training for her 12th marathon.

Magazine websites

Run For Your Life	http://www.runforyourlife.com.au/
Australian Triathlete	http://www.oztri.com.au/
Canadian Running	http://runningmagazine.ca/
IMPACT Magazine	http://www.impactmagazine.ca/